NEW EDITION

Business Basics

Teacher's Book

David Grant and Robert McLarty

Great Clarendon Street, Oxford OX2 6DP

Oxford University Press is a department of the University of Oxford. It furthers the University's objective of excellence in research, scholarship, and education by publishing worldwide in

Oxford New York

Athens Auckland Bangkok Bogotá Buenos Aires Cape Town
Chennai Dar es Salaam Delhi Florence Hong Kong Istanbul
Karachi Kolkata Kuala Lumpur Madrid Melbourne Mexico City
Mumbai Nairobi Paris São Paulo Shanghai Singapore Taipei
Tokyo Toronto Warsaw

with associated companies in Berlin Ibadan

Oxford and Oxford English are registered trade marks of
Oxford University Press in the UK and in certain other countries

© Oxford University Press 2001

The moral rights of the author have been asserted

Database right Oxford University Press (maker)

First published 2001
Second impression 2001

All rights reserved. No part of this publication may be reproduced, stored in a retrieval system, or transmitted, in any form or by any means, without the prior permission in writing of Oxford University Press, or as expressly permitted by law, or under terms agreed with the appropriate reprographics rights organization. Enquiries concerning reproduction outside the scope of the above should be sent to the ELT Rights Department, Oxford University Press, at the address above

You must not circulate this book in any other binding or cover and you must impose this same condition on any acquirer

Photocopying

The Publisher grants permission for the photocopying of those pages marked 'photocopiable' according to the following conditions. Individual purchasers may make copies for their own use or for use by classes that they teach. School purchasers may make copies for use by staff and students, but this permission does not extend to additional schools or branches

Under no circumstances may any part of this book be photocopied for resale

ISBN 0 19 457342 7

Printed in Hong Kong

ACKNOWLEDGEMENTS

The authors and publisher would like to thank the following for their advice and assistance in the preparation of this book:

Ismael Alonso, Mariel Bas, Peter Ball, Carolina Bell, V Bellamy-Tirel, Bozena Blaim, Monique Blais-Algie, Adrian Boz, C Calvert, Maurice Cassidy, A Charbonnier, Helena Chavarria, Joanne Ciercierska, Bob Curtis, the Darby School of Languages, Rome, Rosemary Dessert, Ginette De Fleuriot, Joy Godwin, Sandra Goodall, Glynis Guillaume, Evelyn Ho, James Jacobson, E Jendrych, Barbara Jenike, Blanche Keohane-Vignaux, Avril Kirkham, Erika Knoll-Damm, İbrahim Küçük, Abdurrahman Kurt, Candy Lee, Katarzyna Mucha, Raquel de Nicolas, Catalina de Pagani, F Rees, Roma Robinson, Kenny Rodia, S Rosenman, Jacqueline Rossoni, L Roux, Clementa Sainz, A J Shepherd, Joanne Townsley, Rosina Vega, E De Volder and the teachers of the OLV v/d HAM Isituut, Mechelen, Michael Worman, Mirta V Zampini

Illustrations by Stephan Chabluk

Contents

Introduction		4
Unit 1	**You and your company**	6
Unit 2	**Preparing a trip**	11
Unit 3	**Away on business**	17
Unit 4	**Visiting a company**	22
Unit 5	**New developments**	27
Unit 6	**Arrangements**	32
Unit 7	**Describing and comparing**	37
Unit 8	**Life stories**	42
Unit 9	**Dealing with problems**	47
Unit 10	**People at work**	52
Unit 11	**Getting a job**	57
Unit 12	**The world of work**	62
Photocopiable activities		67
Progress Tests		79
Answer key to Tests		94

Introduction

Business Basics consists of twelve thematically-linked units. Each unit is divided into three sections, each with one or two main teaching points, which may be grammatical, functional, or lexical. Students are given the opportunity to practise language in meaningful contexts.

The course is intended to be used continuously, with a structural and lexical progression from beginning to end. However, units and sections can be presented in a different order, or omitted, according to the specific needs of the students. The book is suitable for in-work students, but may also be used by business English students who have not yet entered the workplace. If students are asked to refer to their own company or professional experience, alternative activities are usually given for those not yet in work.

Course components

The course consists of a **Student's Book**, intended principally for classroom use. This is accompanied by two audio **Cassettes** or **CDs**. The **Workbook** consolidates the key language taught in the Student's Book. The **Teacher's Book** provides section-by-section lesson plans for all the units in the Student's Book. It includes photocopiable pages for extra classroom activities, and five Progress Tests. The **Personal Cassettes** package is an individual resource for students requiring further interactive listening and speaking practice of language taught in the course.

Student's Book

Each section heading shows the main teaching points in four different categories: **Grammar**, **Pronunciation**, **Vocabulary**, and **Communication skills**. These appear in the **Contents pages** for easy reference. Exercises and activities are divided into six different types: **Speaking**, **Listening**, **Reading**, **Writing**, **Vocabulary**, **Pronunciation**. These refer to the main skill or language area being covered, although students may be practising other skills at the same time. New language is always presented through one of these activity types, and summarized in the form of a **Language Note** (see opposite).

Speaking

These activities may be used:

- for initial discussion around a theme
- to assess students' knowledge of a language point
- to provide controlled or freer practice of target language. Students may be in pair work, group or whole class mode, and involved in either role play or discussion.

Listening

These activities give practice in:

- understanding new language in its spoken form
- listening for specific information
- understanding the gist of the passage.

In the interests of building learner confidence, most of the listening texts have been recorded at a measured pace, using a variety of native and non-native speaker accents. Most of the tasks can be accomplished after the passage has been played twice.

Reading

Wherever possible, reading texts have been adapted from authentic sources. They are generally quite short, and are used:

- to present or practise new language or vocabulary
- to practise information-finding or general comprehension
- to provide models for subsequent writing work (letters, faxes, e-mails, etc).

Writing

Students are taught many of the standard expressions used in business correspondence, including CVs and letters of application, and are made aware of some of the differences between formal and informal writing styles. They are also asked to produce short e-mails, faxes, or letters based on models provided. These include giving directions to a visitor or requesting further information.

Vocabulary

These activities extend students' vocabulary in a given lexical area, and give them an opportunity to practise the new terms in both controlled and freer contexts. Emphasis is given to vocabulary learning and storing techniques such as deduction from context, definitions, example sentences, and categorization. The **Glossary** (see opposite) complements the **Vocabulary** activities in the book.

Pronunciation

These exercises give listening and oral practice in sound distinction, word stress, sentence stress, and different forms of word-linking. They are designed to raise awareness of various pronunciation issues, rather than providing a comprehensive grounding in all major aspects. Models are provided on the **Cassettes / CDs** in standard British English.

Language Note

This provides a brief summary of new language with explanatory comments and example sentences. It appears at a point in the unit section where students are ready to see a summary of what they are learning. There is no task attached, but it is usually followed by another activity where the language is practised further. Some unit sections have two **Language Notes**.

The Student's Book also contains the following resources.

Information Files (pages 150–155)

These provide support material for pair work activities involving information exchange, as well as answers to certain quiz or game activities. Students are referred to Files at the relevant point in the unit section.

Language Files (pages 156–162)

This section gives a summary of key structures taught or practised in the book. It complements the **Language Notes** (see above) which appear in the main body of the book. It includes supplementary grammatical information, such as substitution tables for verb tense forms, and overviews of related language points covered in separate unit sections in the book, e.g. social language.

Tapescript (pages 163–171)

This contains the text of all the listening and pronunciation exercises on the **Cassettes / CDs**. Once the original listening task has been completed, the tapescript can be used as a resource for checking answers, searching for examples of vocabulary and grammar items, or reading aloud for pronunciation practice. If students have difficulty in completing a listening task, they can be encouraged to read and listen to the tapescript at the same time. Using the tapescript should not be regarded as a sign of failure.

Glossary (pages 172–175)

This contains definitions of business vocabulary encountered in the course. Many entries include example sentences to show the words in context. Each headword is accompanied by a reference to the unit section in which the word first appears. This enables the **Glossary** to be used by both teachers and students as a systematic revision tool.

Workbook

The Workbook complements the Student's Book with additional practice exercises, primarily for individual work between lessons. Most exercises test only the language presented and practised in the book. However, in a number of reading- and vocabulary-based exercises, students have the opportunity to extend their lexical knowledge beyond terms already learnt in the book. Students are offered a variety of different exercise types, and there are a number of reading texts which, as in the Student's Book, are usually based on authentic sources.

The Workbook includes a complete **Answer key**. Students should be encouraged to check their work themselves and, in the case of wrong answers, to think about why they were wrong. This also saves lesson time when going over homework, since it avoids teachers having to go over every answer.

Teacher's Book

The Teacher's Book gives detailed lesson notes for each unit section. Most lesson plans offer ideas for warm-up activities, and a number of them have practical ideas for follow-up work. There are also helpful tips at intervals for organization and layout of board work. The step-by-step notes follow the order of activities in the Student's Book. The teaching objective is given for each activity, and there are indications as to whether the task should be done as a whole class, in groups, or in pairs. Answers to each exercise are provided immediately after the teaching notes for that activity.

The Teacher's Book also contains the following elements.

Photocopiable activities (pages 67–78)

There is one activity for each unit of the Student's Book. Each gives freer practice in the main language points of the unit. They are generally lighter activities involving sharing of information or problem-solving in either pairs or groups. Teaching notes for each activity appear at the end of the corresponding unit in the Teacher's Book.

Photocopiable Progress Tests (pages 79–93)

There are five Progress Tests. The first four test language taught in Units 1–3, 4–6, 7–9 and 10–12. Test 5 acts as revision for the whole course. Each test gives a total mark out of 100. Exercises are vocabulary-, grammar-, or functionally-based. An **Answer key** appears on pages 94–96.

Personal Cassettes

These are available in a blister pack incorporating two **audio cassettes** and a **Pocket Book**. They are designed for students working individually who want to develop their listening and speaking skills.

The cassettes follow closely the syllabus and structure of *Business Basics*, providing extra listening and speaking practice in most of the language points taught. Each unit has five sections that provide freer practice as the unit progresses. Students are asked to repeat sentences, to transform structures, to take part in dialogues, or just to listen for pleasure. All instructions are on the cassette. The **Pocket Book** contains a glossary, and tapescripts for all the listening material, so students can check anything they don't understand without the help of a teacher.

Unit 1 | You and your company

1.1 People in business

A [1]

This exercise focuses on the present simple and the verb *be*. Ask students to look at the photo of Lorella and the map of Italy, and to read the initial rubric. Elicit where Lorella is from and what her job is.

1 Check that students understand the information they need. Play the tape once or twice as necessary so that they can complete the task. Check answers with the whole class.

Name:	Lorella Braglia
Nationality:	Italian
Home:	Reggio Emilia, Italy
Age:	30
Company:	Dielle
Job:	main designer
Languages:	English, Italian

2 If appropriate, write the present simple tense of the verb *be* on the board (you can add the contractions later in the lesson). Play the tape and let students complete the sentences individually. Check answers with the whole class. Point out that the third person singular form of the present simple takes an *s*.

1 is	2 lives	3 is	4 works	5 is	6 are		
7 speak	8 work						

Elicit the questions used by the journalist for name, nationality, and job, and write them on the board.

> What is her name?
> Where is she from?
> What is her job?

Practise the questions orally and then substitute *your* for *her*, and *are you* for *is she*. Refer students to the Language Note on page 7. Point out the contracted forms and add them to your questions on the board.

B

This exercise gives students the chance to speak to and meet each other.

1 Let students ask and answer the questions with a partner and then move around the class, asking at least three other people. Monitor and correct where appropriate. Follow up with some *yes / no* practice around the room. Use prompt cards with different nationalities / jobs written on them.

2 Ask students to introduce each other to the class, using the example in the book.

C [2]

This exercise consolidates practice of the present simple form of regular verbs and the verb *be*.

1 Let students work in pairs to complete the article. The verbs are provided in the correct form in the box and the first letter is given. Check answers with the whole class, then ask general comprehension questions about the article, keeping to the present simple.

1	is	9	live
2	works	10	are
3	designs	11	travel
4	presents	12	do
5	makes	13	plays
6	uses	14	play
7	employs	15	eat
8	produces		

2 Read the rubric, then play the tape for students to do the task individually.

/s/	makes works presents
/z/	is employs designs
/ɪz/	uses produces

3 Play the tape again for students to check. Point out the different pronunciations on a phonemic chart if you have one. Then let students work in pairs to read the passage aloud.

Language Note

This summarizes the rule for using the present simple. Read through with students and elicit other example sentences.

D [3]

By this stage in the lesson you will probably have had to spell several words so this exercise aims to introduce, revise, or check the alphabet.

1 Before listening to the tape, check students understand the phonemic symbols in the table. If necessary, offer them similar sounding words such as gr**ey**, gr**ee**n, r**e**d, yell**ow**, wh**i**te, bl**u**e, and d**a**rk blue. Play the tape for students to fill in the table individually.

2 Play the tape again for students to check. Practise saying the letters in groupings and in alphabetical order. Do one or two dictations of words in the room such as T-A-B-L-E, or C-H-A-I-R. Ask students to spell some words themselves just to be at ease with the letters. Practise the question *How do you spell that / it?*

3 Let students work in pairs to do the task. If they are all in the same school / town, substitute with other names.

4 Teach the expression *What does it stand for?* by using a well-known abbreviation or acronym such as WWW (world wide web). Let students do the activity in pairs and then feed back with the whole class.

EU:	European Union
WC:	water-closet
Plc:	Public Limited Company
UK:	United Kingdom
USA:	United States of America
UN:	United Nations
IBM:	International Business Machines
MBA:	Masters of Business Administration
VAT:	Value Added Tax
CEO:	Chief Executive Officer

E [4]

This exercise continues practice of the alphabet. Play the tape once and ask students to write down the names they hear. When checking answers, ask if anyone heard the whole sentence.

1 BA	3 HP	5 E. Sanz	7 BA
2 GM	4 BASF	6 AOL	8 FBI

F [5]

This listening and speaking exercise consolidates the language covered so far in the unit.

1 Encourage students to listen only for the required information and not to worry about understanding every word. Play [5a] once. Elicit any information heard by students and write it on the board. Play [5a] again for students to complete the task. This method encourages the weaker listeners and is quite supportive early on in the course.

Name:	Gonzague Lepoutre
Company:	UBS
Job:	Human Resources Manager
Nationality:	French
Home:	England, near Oxford

2 This exercise is best done as a class. Ask students to write down their responses as you play [5b] the first time. On the second playing, invite verbal responses.

Language Note
Read through with students and practise the phrases.

Optional extra activity
Ask students to work in fours with A introducing B and C to D, and so on. Use real names, or invented ones if the class is monolingual. You can prepare identity cards with information similar to the person in **F** **1** – giving name, nationality, job, etc. The class can then introduce themselves and meet each other.

G [6]

1 This listening activity is an information search. Read the rubric, then play the tape once for students to fill in the table. Check answers with the whole class.

1 journalist	5 SAP
2 Business Monthly	6 Japanese
3 Italian	7 software engineer
4 consultant	8 SAP

2 The second listening requires more detailed answers. Play the tape again and ask students to fill in the gaps and check in pairs. Then ask them to act out the completed dialogue in groups of four. Monitor, and correct where necessary.

1	let me introduce
2	do you do
3	meet
4	do you do
5	This is
6	to meet you
7	to meet you too
8	software engineer
9	a journalist. I work

1.2 Talking about your company

A

See how much vocabulary about companies students already know. Look at the pictures and brainstorm associated vocabulary. Do not worry about accuracy at this stage, the aim is to revive passive vocabulary and to show the class that the concepts are the same even if the language is different.

Ask students to do the exercise in pairs and then check back with you. Then ask them to rewrite the sentences using other words, e.g. *The head office of Microsoft is in Seattle.*

1 head office	5 factories
2 markets	6 employees
3 Sales	7 product
4 competitors	8 customers

B 7

This exercise is an extensive listening. Students have to find out some key information about Nokia.

① Put the headings on the board and play the tape once. Pool information, and if necessary listen a second time.

Company:	Nokia
Activity:	produce / sell mobile phones, build base stations
Head office:	Helsinki
Research centre:	Tampere
Employees:	53,000
Languages:	Finnish, English
Major markets:	China, US, Europe
Main competitors:	Motorola, Ericsson
Advertising:	TV, magazines, buses, sports sponsorship

② Ask students to look at the incomplete questions from the listening text. See if they can remember the questions, or form them from the answers. Play the tape again so they can listen and check.

1 does the company do
2 is the head office
3 Where are your
4 How ... people do you employ
5 languages do you speak
6 Where ... advertise

C

This exercise practises making and answering questions. If necessary refer students to the Language Note, pointing out the importance of *do / does*.

① Half the class should look at File I on page 151 and the other half at File O on page 152. They should prepare questions with a partner, then form A / B pairs to complete the task. Monitor, noting any particularly good language and any mistakes that you can look at afterwards.

② Still in pairs, students ask questions about their partner's company. Give them time to write a description and then let them report back orally to the rest of the class.

D

① This exercise helps students to distinguish between verbs and nouns. First, ask students to cover the sentences and look at the pairs of words in *italics*. Elicit possible sentences about Nokia using these words. Then let students do the exercise in pairs and check back with you.

1 advertises; advertisements
2 produces; products
3 sells; sales
4 employees; employs
5 competitors; competes
6 suppliers; supplies

② This could be set as a homework task along with ③.

③ This helps students learn about vocabulary building and how one word can be the source of three or four more words in the same family. If you wish, you can highlight the importance of word stress, particularly how it changes according to length and class (verb or noun).

1 salesman / saleswoman / salesperson
2 competition
3 advertise
4 unemployment
5 employee
6 production

E 8

① Write the table on the board and elicit answers from the class. If there is time, students can add more items and countries. Check pronunciation of the nationalities, paying particular attention to word stress.

2 Play the tape for students to check answers. Check students understand the idea of a stress pattern, by looking at the examples on the page. Play the tape again and ask students to put the words in the correct column.

●	●○	○●	●○○	○○●	○●○○
France	Spanish	Brazil	Italy	Japanese	Brazilian
French	China	Japan	Germany	Portuguese	Italian
Spain	German	Chinese	Portugal		Australia
			Mexico		Australian
			Mexican		

F 9

This exercise focuses on leisure activities.

1 The questions can be predicted from the text and then checked by listening.

2 Play the tape again so students can complete the answers.

1 What do you do at the weekends?	I often go to my cabin near Lake Pukkala.
2 What do you do there?	I swim or play tennis.
3 Who do you play with?	My sons.
4 Where do you swim?	In the lake.
5 What do you do in the evenings?	I listen to music or take a sauna.

3 This pair-work activity practises *Wh-* question forms in the present simple.

G

This exercise provides speaking practice.

1 Give students a minute or two to prepare and then let them take it in turns to talk about themselves. Ignore mistakes and encourage speaking rather than reading from notes.

2 Students report back about their partner. Note mistakes and correct them later.

1.3 Company facts and figures

A

1 Depending on the level of your group you may need to revise numbers. As a warmer, dictate ten different numbers. Choose numbers where there might be confusion: 12, 20, 13, 30, etc. and make the numbers longer and longer. Check answers, then ask students to say the numbers and do the matching task.

| 1 75,000,000 |
| 2 805,602 |
| 3 1,280 |
| 4 26,836,000 |
| 5 432 |

2 This activity reinforces some of the vocabulary from Unit 1.2 and teaches some new words which occur in the listening comprehension in the next exercise. Let students work individually or in pairs, and then check back with you. Encourage the use of monolingual dictionaries if they have a problem understanding or pronouncing a word.

1 located	5 competitors
2 products	6 outlets
3 employs	7 subsidiary
4 turnover	8 market share

B 10

The class will listen to a short presentation three times, with different tasks each time. Again, try to show your class that they can listen and understand without needing to understand every word.

1 Play 10a once and check understanding by asking students to answer *true* or *false*.

| 1 F | 2 F | 3 T | 4 F | 5 T |

2 Check students can pronounce the numbers correctly so they know what they are listening out for. Play 10a again, then check answers.

| 1 e | 2 f | 3 b | 4 g | 5 a | 6 d | 7 c |

3 The final activity focuses on the expressions used in the presentation. Students will be using this language later so they need to master it. Play 10a for students to complete the extracts. Check answers with the whole class.

| 1 here; brief; company |
| 2 first part; looks at; last part; talk about |
| 3 First; Let's start |
| 4 let's look at |
| 5 have; questions |

Language Note

Read through with students and practise the language as necessary.

C

This exercise is based on the Swatch group. See if anyone is wearing or owns one of their watches.

1 Ask students to read the notes, and check comprehension and vocabulary. Then ask them to close their books, and brainstorm on the board all the information they can recall. Prompt them where necessary. When you have a full board, ask them to look at the information again and try to organize it into topic areas.

2 Let students do this task in pairs as it follows on directly from **1**. Check answers with the whole class.

Organization / Structure:	1, 3, 10
Location / Distribution:	5, 11
Products:	2, 4, 6, 9, 14
Sales:	8, 13
Future plans:	7, 12

3 The point of this task is to illustrate how notes can be expanded into full sentences when you are making a presentation. Let students work in pairs before checking back with you.

4 Students should now be ready to make a presentation. If they are hesitant, let them work in pairs or threes. Refer them to the Language Note, which gives useful phrases for presenting a company.

Optional extra activity

Ask students to find as many facts as they can about a company of their choice (the Internet is a good source of information). They can then compile a profile of this company, which will be useful for the second activity in **E**.

D 11

This exercise is designed to help students with fluency in spoken English.

1 Go through the example, then play the tape for students to complete the task.

2 Play the tape again for students to check.

> 1 <u>Where</u> do you <u>work</u>?
> 2 How <u>much</u> does he <u>earn</u>?
> 3 <u>What</u> does she <u>do</u>?
> 4 He <u>doesn't</u> <u>speak</u> <u>English</u>.
> 5 Does she <u>work</u> here <u>now</u>? <u>Yes</u>, she <u>does</u>.
> 6 Do you <u>use</u> a <u>PC</u>? <u>Yes</u>, I <u>do</u>.

E 12

To end the unit, students are asked to make a short presentation on their own company.

1 Students listen to the questions and answer about their own company. Make sure those who don't work choose a company they know well.

2 Students can then prepare their presentation as a homework task. In the next lesson, let students give their presentations in small groups or to the whole class.

Photocopiable activity (page 67)

This provides further practice in introductions and small talk. Ask students to work in groups of three.

All three passengers are in a plane and one is meeting the other two for the first time. Ask groups to prepare a conversation and then practise it in pairs. Swap roles after a while to allow each student to role-play passenger A. Invite some groups to act out the conversation in front of the others.

Unit 2 | Preparing a trip

2.1 Choosing a hotel

A

This exercise focuses on key hotel vocabulary. As a warmer, ask students to write down the names of three well-known hotels. Choose one yourself and spell it aloud slowly, for students to guess the name. The first person to call out the name has to finish spelling it. They should then continue in pairs with the names they chose.

1 Let students work on this individually, then check answers with the whole class.

> 1 shuttle bus   3 swimming pool   5 electronic safe
> 2 car park   4 business centre 6 conference rooms

2 Elicit examples, and build up a list on the board.

> Other services: fitness room / gymnasium, hairdresser, shops, restaurant, bars, laundry

As a follow-up, you could ask students in pairs to list facilities which would be particularly useful for:

- a business hotel in the city centre (*conference rooms, business centre, secretarial service*, etc.)
- a holiday hotel by the sea (*laundry, outdoor swimming pool, souvenir shop*, etc.)

B

This exercise is a lead-in to *there is* and *there are*. The standard letter phrases used here are dealt with in **G**. Refer students to the letter and note. Ask them to find:
- a date
- two fax numbers
- the name of two hotels
- the name of Sylvie Dutertre's secretary.

Then ask them to read the letter in more detail and answer the three questions individually.

> 1 To the Century Park and Royal Princess Hotels
> 2 a
> 3 a single room with a bath

C

This exercise introduces *there is* and *there are*.

1 Elicit / teach questions students could ask in a hotel in the following situations:

- they have a car (*Is there a car park?*)
- they like swimming (*Is there a swimming pool?*)
- they like shopping (*Are there any shops?*)

Then refer students to the Language Note. Point out that *is*, *isn't*, and *a* become *are*, *aren't*, and *any* in the plural. Do the exercise together, then let students work in pairs on a list of other questions they might ask in the same situation.

> 1 Is there a business centre?
> 2 Are there any conference rooms?
> 3 Is there a shuttle bus to the airport?

2 One side of the class looks at the Century Park information on page 19, the other at File C on page 150. Focus on the pictures, and ask what facilities they think there are in the hotel. Then ask them to read the list of facilities with a partner and make sentences with *there is / are*.

When they have finished, form A / B pairs to ask and answer their questions. They should note down their partner's answers. Feed back by asking questions like:

- Which hotel has more rooms / restaurants, etc.?
- Which hotel has / doesn't have a coffee shop, etc.?

D 13

This introduces polite requests using *can*, *could*, and *may*.

1 Check comprehension of the vocabulary in the booking form. With a stronger group, you could start by asking them to improvise a dialogue between a hotel receptionist and a caller who wants to reserve a room. Play the dialogue twice if necessary. Let students compare answers in pairs before checking back with you.

Name:	Mr Gervais
Company:	CMC (Cambridge Management Consulting)
Type of room:	single
Date of arrival:	Monday 1st November
Date of departure:	Thursday 4th November (3 nights)
Confirmation by:	fax

2 Let students complete this individually, then play the tape to check.

> Receptionist: 2 and 3   Caller: 1, 4, and 5

3 See if any students can remember any of the responses, then listen to check.

> 1 Certainly, sir.
> 3 I'm afraid I'm not in my office.
> 4 Yes, of course. That's fine.

Language Note
Give students a few minutes to read this. Point out that *can* and *could* are used both with *I* and *you*, but that *may* is only used with *I*. Ask them which responses are positive and which are negative. To check their understanding of *polite*, elicit other situations in which you would use these expressions, e.g. with your boss, with a customer, with a stranger on a train or plane.

E [14]
This exercise gives students practice in making and responding to requests.

1 Point out that for some gaps there is more than one possibility. Go through the first two lines together, then let students continue alone before comparing answers in pairs.

> 1 Excuse me   4 Could you   7 I'm sorry
> 2 Can I   5 of course   8 Could you
> 3 I'm afraid   6 could I   9 certainly

2 See if students can work this out before they listen, then play the tape to check their answers to **1**.

> Conversation 1 is face to face
> Conversation 2 is on the telephone

3 Do question 1 together, then let students work in pairs, taking turns to make the request. Alternatively, they can do the exercise twice, swapping roles the second time. Then ask individual pairs to perform each dialogue to the class. Try to elicit a positive and negative response for each request.

> 1 Can I / Could you open the window, please?
> 2 Can I / Could I smoke?
> 3 Can / Could you tell me the time, please?
> 4 May / Can / Could I use your mobile phone, please?
> 5 May / Can / Could I have a glass of water, please?
> 6 Can / Could you call me tomorrow morning?
> 7 May / Can / Could I look at your newspaper, please?
> 8 Can / Could you bring me a coffee, please?

F [15a]

1 Start by modelling *the* and *think*. Demonstrate the /ð/ sound by asking them to put their fingers on their throat so that they can feel the vibration. With /θ/ there is no vibration. Students whose mother tongue does not distinguish these sounds will find this difficult and they will need to practise. Play [15a] for students to listen and put the words in the box according to their sound.

/θ/	think	bath	thank	theatre	month	three
	thirty					
/ð/	the	this	that	other	there	

Students listen to [15b] and repeat the sentences.

G

This exercise introduces the standard phrases for starting and finishing letters.

1 Students read the fax again, then answer the questions in pairs. Feed back with the whole class, pointing out that all these expressions are used in more formal letters. You might like to point out that in letters to people we know well, we use less formal expressions, e.g. *Dear Sophie, Best regards, Can you ...?*

> 1 She starts 'Dear Sir or Madam' and finishes 'Yours faithfully' because she is writing to a hotel rather than a particular person.
> 2 I would be grateful if you could ...
> 3 I look forward to hearing from you.

2 When students have finished writing their letters individually, ask them to compare their version in pairs.

> **Model answer:**
>
> Dear Mrs Glens
> I have an appointment with you at the Compaq Computer Corporation in Houston on Friday 13th June. I would be grateful if you could send me a road map of Houston. Could you also confirm the exact time of my meeting?
> I look forward to hearing from you.
> Yours sincerely
> Sylvie Dutertre

H

This revises the vocabulary of the section and introduces word chains, which are a very useful technique for storing vocabulary to describe processes. Ask students what they do when they arrive at work / school, e.g. say hello to colleagues, buy a coffee, go to the office. Build up a short word chain on the board, then ask them to do the same for arriving at a hotel.

1 Students complete the chain individually; the order they choose will depend on their personal preference. Feed back, correcting only when the order is illogical.

Possible answer:
1 key	4 phone call	7 shower
2 lift	5 suitcase	8 restaurant
3 room	6 fitness room	9 satellite TV

2 Ask students to match the verbs and nouns, then check back with the whole class.

You make a reservation, park in the car park, check in at / go to reception, collect / take your key, take the lift, go to your room, make a phone call, unpack your suitcase, use / go to the fitness room, take a shower, eat in the restaurant, watch satellite TV, go to bed.

2.2 Flying out

A

As a warmer, ask students for any words they know relating to air travel. Make a list on the board. Refer students to the pictures. Point out that Odil's plane leaves in under two hours. Check understanding of *check-in time* and ask them to find a *flight timetable* and a *watch*. They then work through the questions in pairs. Monitor and go through answers with the whole class, but do not correct errors at this point.

1 4.45 p.m. on Sunday
2 the Sunday flight at 18.00 (BA870)
3 two hours and 25 minutes
4 yes
5 a on the watch
  b arrival time of second flight on timetable
  c departure time of third flight

Language Note
Point out that the first two ways of saying the time are more common, and used equally often. To check comprehension, elicit and write on the board a table of equivalents as follows.

17.05
five past five / five oh five p.m. / seventeen oh five
17.15
quarter past five / five fifteen p.m. / seventeen fifteen
17.30
half past five / five thirty p.m. / seventeen thirty
17.45
quarter to six / five forty-five p.m. / seventeen forty-five
17.50
ten to six / five fifty p.m. / seventeen fifty

Then go over students' mistakes from **A**, and ask them to correct them in the light of what they have learnt.

B 16

1 Students work in groups of three to practise saying the times in one of the ways outlined above. Feed back, choosing a different person from each group to give the alternative ways of saying each time.

10.00	ten o' clock in the morning (a.m.)
19.00	seven o' clock in the evening (p.m.) or nineteen hundred
04.15	four fifteen or quarter past four in the morning (a.m.)
15.15	three fifteen or quarter past three in the afternoon (p.m.) or fifteen fifteen
09.20	nine twenty or twenty past nine in the morning (a.m.)
19.20	seven twenty or twenty past seven in the evening (p.m.) or nineteen twenty
09.30	nine thirty or half past nine in the morning (a.m.)
17.30	five thirty or half past five in the afternoon (p.m.) or seventeen thirty
03.45	three forty-five or quarter to four in the morning (a.m.)
14.45	two forty-five or quarter to three in the afternoon (p.m.) or fourteen forty-five
09.50	nine fifty or ten to ten in the morning (a.m.)
22.50	ten fifty or ten to eleven in the evening (p.m.) or twenty-two fifty

2 Students hear three short extracts in which the speakers use the different ways of saying the time. Play the tape twice, allowing students to compare answers before checking with the whole class.

1	15.15	17.30	19.00
2	09.20	09.50	
3	14.45		

3 Students complete the 'You' column, writing the times as numbers. Then elicit a couple of examples of the questions they have to ask their partner (*What time do you ...?*) before completing the activity in pairs.

C

Half the class should look at Student A's information, and the other half at File P on page 152. They should prepare their questions with a partner, then form A / B pairs for the role-play. Point out that the 24-hour clock is acceptable here as they are talking about flight schedules. Monitor, noting any mistakes. Then ask students which flight they reserved (it should be Saturday, Sunday, or Monday). Write the mistakes you noted on the board and ask students to correct them.

D 17

This activity introduces the language of time, distance, and frequency. Focus on the photos of Warsaw and ask if anybody knows it. What views of their own home town are usually shown in tourist brochures?

1 Ask students to suggest possible answers. Play the tape, and let students compare answers in pairs before checking back with you.

1	10 km	6	8.00 a.m.
2	25 minutes	7	6.00 p.m.
3	half an hour (30 minutes)	8	11.00 a.m.
4	5.30 a.m.	9	2.00 p.m.
5	11.00 p.m.	10	8.00 or 9.00 a.m.

2 Students may have problems with *When is it open?* and *When does it open?* Similarly, *How long ...?*, *How far ...?* and *How often ...?* are often confused. If so, they should use the Language Note to help them complete their answers. Then play the tape again to check.

| 1 d | 2 b | 3 a | 4 e | 5 c |

Language Note

Read through with students. Then return to 2 above. Ask them to cover a–e and reproduce the answers using the notes in 1. Finally, elicit other questions for each of the forms, e.g. *How often do we have an English lesson? How long does it take to go from A to B?*

Optional extra activity

For extra practice, ask students to write down four or five sentences about themselves using one of the frequency expressions, e.g. *I go to the theatre three or four times a year.* Each student then reads the first part of each sentence, e.g. *I go to the theatre ...* to a partner, who must guess what the frequency expression is.

E

Do the first question together, then ask students to finish writing the questions. Feed back with the whole class, then students complete the questionnaire in pairs.

> **Questions:**
> – How far is it from your home to your company / school?
> – How long does it take to get there?
> – When is reception open / How long is reception open for?
> – When / How often is your company / school closed for holidays?
> – When do you usually start / finish work?
> – How often do you work after 6.00 p.m. / at weekends?

F 18

1 This practises distinguishing easily-confused numbers. In pairs, students take turns to say one of the numbers, while their partner points to the one they said. Point out that the stress generally falls on the second syllable for the numbers ending *teen*, and on the first syllable for the numbers ending *ty*, e.g. *thir**teen** / **thir**ty, four**teen** / **for**ty*. Model the different numbers, and ask students to repeat.

2 Play the tape once without stopping. Let students compare answers in pairs, then play the tape again sentence by sentence to check.

| 1 | 70 | 3 | 3.15 | 5 | 14 hours | 7 | 16 minutes |
| 2 | 18 km | 4 | 30 | 6 | 90 | | |

G

For this free-practice activity, pair people from different countries. In a monolingual group, pair students from different home towns. Monitor the pairs, asking students to correct themselves if you hear any mistakes in the target language.

Optional extra activity

Ask students to produce a poster incorporating all the information asked for, including photos of places of interest, timetables, tourist leaflets, etc.

2.3 Arriving

A

This activity teaches some basic expressions to do with air travel. Remind students of the list of words you produced as a lead-in to Unit 2.1. Write on the board the first letters of the words they noted, and ask them to complete them without looking back at their notes.

① Students work in pairs. Feed back with the whole class.

1 i	3 f	5 d	7 a	9 h
2 j	4 g	6 e	8 c	10 b

② Students practise the phrases in pairs.

B 19

This listening activity introduces the concept of countable and uncountable nouns.

① Tell students each conversation takes place in one of the areas mentioned in **A**. Play the tape and let students compare answers in pairs before checking back with you.

1 passport control   **2** customs

② Play the tape again, stopping at the end of each target sentence.

many: 1 and 4   *much*: 2 and 3

③ Elicit the answer from the whole class. If they need help, ask them which nouns are plural, and which are singular.

How much is used with singular (uncountable) nouns.
How many is used with plural (countable) nouns.

C

① Ask students to complete the questions in pairs, and also to try and predict the answers.

many: 1 3 5 6   *much*: 2 4 7 8

② Refer students to File D on page 150. If some students have the wrong answer and don't understand why, ask those who were correct to explain their answers by referring to the text. Ask them what goods they can (or can't) bring into their own country, and in what quantity.

1 h	2 a	3 g	4 c	5 d	6 b	7 f	8 e

Language Note

Read through with students. To check comprehension, write the table below on the board for students to complete with words from the example sentences. Then elicit sentences with *suitcase(s)*, *book(s)*, *advice*, and *wine*, each of which should include one of the countable or uncountable expressions, e.g. *How much wine is there?* Refer to the Language file on page 156.

[C]	[U]
a / an	some
How many?	How much?
(not) many	(not) much
any / some	any / some
suitcase	advice
book	wine

D

This highlights some of the most commonly confused nouns, particularly *information, money, luggage,* and *news*, which are countable in many other languages.

① Do the exercise together, reinforcing the countable / uncountable distinction by pointing out that we can say, for example, *a shop / two shops*, but we cannot say *a luggage / two luggages*. Point out also that although *news* has a final *s*, it is uncountable. As an alternative, you could ask students to find the answers in a dictionary.

1 C	3 U	5 C	7 U	9 U
2 C	4 U	6 C	8 C	10 U

② Remind students that we use *some* in affirmative sentences, and *any* in questions and negatives. (Exceptions such as offers, e.g. *Would you like some coffee?* are not included here). Students complete the task individually, then compare with a partner before checking back with you.

1 any	3 some	5 any	7 any; a
2 any	4 a; some	6 a	8 some

E 20

① This introduces the *have / have got* distinction. Listen once, and let students compare notes before checking back with you.

1 no, he doesn't
2 a single room with bath and shower

2 Stop the tape after each sentence to let students complete the gaps. Point out that there are two different ways of asking the same question. The short answer uses the same form as the question.
e.g. *Do you have ...? No, I **don't**.* or *Yes, I **do.***
or *Has it got ...? No, it **hasn't**.* or *Yes, it **has**.*

Language Note
Students read this, then suggest further questions a guest in a hotel might ask with *have* or *have got*, e.g. *Have all the rooms got TV? Do you have a restaurant?*
With stronger students, you could ask them to transform sentences from the *there is / are* form to the *have / have got* form and vice versa.
e.g. *There are three restaurants in the hotel = The hotel has / has got three restaurants.*
Is there a hairdresser? = Does the hotel have / has the hotel got a hairdresser?

F

1 Ask students to read the dialogue aloud with a partner, then repeat it substituting *have* for *have got* and vice versa.

2 With a weaker group, start by eliciting the questions from the whole class. During the pair work, monitor the pairs and ask students to correct themselves when you hear wrong use of the target expressions.

Possible questions:
1 Do you have any customers in the US?
2 How many employees does your company have / has your company got?
3 Have you got any staff in other countries?
4 Does your company have any factories abroad?
5 How many staff do you have in the head office?
6 Do you have many competitors?
7 Has your company got a big market share?
8 Do you have a research department?

G

A mind map is another useful way of storing vocabulary. Like the word chain in Unit 2.1, it works on the principle that we learn new words by association with other words.

1 Students complete the task in pairs. Feed back with the whole class.

Missing words:
Hotel room: *shower*
Business centre: *conference room*
Other services: *car park*
Airport: before flight: *departure lounge*
 during flight: *land*
Arranging a trip: *confirm*
Free time: *to go sightseeing; department stores*

2 Let students look back to find other words from Unit 2 to fit in the different categories. The second task could be set for homework. Start off on the board, eliciting the initial keyword, e.g. *companies*, and sub-categories, e.g. *jobs, nationalities, company structure, business verbs, facts and figures* and one or two examples for each category. Then leave students to do the rest themselves – a mind map is most effective when it reflects the student's own thought processes. In the next lesson, ask students to compare their completed mind maps.

H

This activity is an opportunity to revise vocabulary from the whole unit. Write the word *fizz* on the board, and begin by giving several models, with students guessing the words.
e.g. *You take the fizz to get from the airport to the hotel.* (shuttle bus)
I arrive at the hotel and I go to fizz to get my room key. (reception)
Then elicit a couple of examples from students for the whole class to guess. They can continue the activity as a whole class or in groups or pairs.

Photocopiable activity (page 68)

This provides further practice in hotel vocabulary, requests, time, distance, and frequency. Give half the class Students A's information and the other half Student B's. Tell them that they will have two conversations, one as a hotel receptionist, and the other as a guest. Have them prepare with a partner the questions they need to ask as the guest. Then ask them to read the receptionist's information and deal with any problems of vocabulary.

Then form Student A and B pairs. Monitor the activity, asking students to self-correct if you hear any mistakes.

Unit 3 | Away on business

3.1 Finding your way

A

This exercise introduces the language for giving directions. As a warmer, give some directions orally to your students and elicit what the destination is. If they are all from your town, give directions from your school to another well-known place in the town. If not, give instructions to get from your classroom to another room / office in your school.

1 Refer students to the map and elicit what other famous places they know in New York. Then ask them to read the letter and tell you its purpose. Let them answer the three questions individually, comparing answers in pairs before checking back with you. Elicit the contextual clues which show that Vernon is coming on foot: he's coming out of the station; the reference to *walk*; there's no mention of a car park.

> **1** Friday 13 June   **2** on foot

2 Students work in pairs, then check back with you.

> **Position:** on your left, on the next corner, on the left, across from, on Fifth Avenue
> **Direction:** turn left, walk up …, take the third right, go straight on down the street, past Macy's, cross Broadway, continue straight on down

B

This exercise focuses first on prepositions of place, then of movement, giving controlled practice of each.

1 Ask students to read the Language Note. If appropriate, illustrate the prepositions on the board with simple diagrams (as in the Language File on page 160) and elicit the correct preposition. Let students complete the questions in pairs, and then do a whole-class feedback.

> **1** A; B is in / on Liberty Avenue, on the right, next to the bank and opposite / across from the post office; C is on Liberty Avenue, on the corner, opposite / across from the bank

> **2** C. In A, the restaurant is on the third floor. The business centre is on the second floor, above Reception and below the restaurant.
> In B, the restaurant is on the second floor, below Reception and above the business centre.
> **3** A. In B, there is a bus in front of the car and a lorry behind. In C, the bus and the lorry are in front of the car.

Optional extra activity
Refer students back to the map of New York in **A**, and ask them to write sentences, using prepositions, to describe the relative position of different landmarks e.g. *Herald Square is between Macy's and the Empire State Building.*

2 Ask students to read the Language Note, and to trace the route in pairs. After doing a whole-class feedback, add the relevant diagrams to the board, again eliciting the prepositions they correspond to.

> You're on the 102nd floor of the Empire State Building.

3 Students work in pairs, then check back with you.

C [21]

1 Refer students to the floor plan, and answer any queries about vocabulary. Ask a few initial checking questions to elicit some more sentences with prepositions. Then refer students to the questions, and play the tape once. Let them compare answers, then play again to check.

> **1** He's in the right building, but on the 4th floor.
> **2** the 14th floor

2 Demonstrate the task first, making sure to indicate which lift / elevator you are starting at. Then let students work in pairs. Monitor, asking them to correct themselves or each other if they make mistakes.

D

This exercise examines formal and informal letter styles and provides further practice of the language of directions, this time in written form.

1 Ask students to look again at the letter in **A**. Explain that Leanne uses an informal style because she knows Vernon well. Ask them to identify any expressions which they think are informal. Then ask them to complete the task individually. Let them compare answers before checking back with you.

1 Dear Vernon	4 Have a safe journey ...
2 Here are instructions ...	5 Best regards
3 Give me a call ...	

2 This can be done in class or set as a homework task. You may like to ask one half of the class to write an informal letter, and the other a formal one. The two versions can then be compared later, with students' checking each other's work for appropriacy of style.

E **22**

1 Play the tape and ask students to repeat each word, first in chorus and then individually. If they have problems distinguishing the sounds, model the pairs of words yourself, exaggerating the 'longness' of the /iː/ sound and the 'shortness' of the /ɪ/. Then play a dictation game where you model the words in random order, and students write them down.

2 Let students do this in pairs, then do a whole-class feedback, asking individual students to repeat the sentences.

Language Note
Students have already used the imperative in giving directions. The Language Note introduces it as a grammatical point, showing other functions it fulfils. Give students time to read it, then elicit / teach other examples of offers (e.g. *Please sit down.*) and advice (e.g. *Don't drink the water*).

F

Before reading the text, ask students why travelling by plane can be very tiring, e.g. change of hour / time zone going from one country to another, not sleeping well, no exercise on plane. Then refer students to the rubric. Go through the example and ask them to read the rest of the text individually and complete the task. Let them compare in pairs before checking back with you.

1 Plan	6 Wear
2 Do	7 Drink
3 Check	8 Don't drink
4 Don't go	9 Stand up
5 Leave	10 don't stay

3.2 Going out

A

This exercise introduces some common verb–noun collocations used for talking about free-time interests. As a warmer, ask students to make three lists: *Things I do on holiday*, *Things I do at weekends*, *Things I do in the evenings*. Help with any vocabulary they need.

1 Explain any unfamiliar terms in the list of activities. Then ask them to complete the table individually. Let them compare answers in pairs before doing a whole-class feedback.

play:	tennis / golf / football / squash
go:	skiing / sailing / sightseeing / cycling / jogging / shopping
have:	a meal in a restaurant / a drink after work
go to:	the cinema / the theatre / the gym / the opera
do:	DIY / karate

2 Answer these questions with the whole class.

| 1 have | 2 go | 3 play | 4 go to |

3 Start by doing an example dialogue with one of the stronger students in the class, adding as many follow-up questions as you can, which the student then answers. Then do the same with another student, but this time invite the rest of the class to contribute the follow-up questions. Finally, ask students to circulate, asking and answering questions. Ask them to make notes on the answers they get so they can then report back to the whole class afterwards.

Language Note
Highlight the *like / would like* distinction by writing the following mini-dialogue on the board.

| A: Do you like to go for a drink after work? |
| B: Yes, that's a good idea. What time? |

Ask students to find the mistake. They may suggest *going* instead of *to go*, in which case you should point out that the response would be different (ask them what it would be). When they have identified the mistake, refer them to the information in the Language Note. Point out that we nearly always use the contracted form of *would like* in the affirmative.

B

1 Do this as a whole-class activity.

> **General interests:** Do you like volleyball?
> **Invitation:** Would you like to play this evening?

2 Do an example dialogue with a stronger student. Choose a different situation from those indicated, e.g. *pizza / go to an Italian restaurant?* Then let students work in pairs, taking it in turns to make or accept / refuse an invitation. When they have finished, ask different pairs to act out their conversation.

C [23]

1 Play the tape once, and let students compare answers with a partner. Play again if necessary, then do a whole-class feedback.

> Monique Dumont called you re your trip to France. Can you call her back on 33-2-51-25-89-74.

2 Let students complete this individually, then compare answers with a partner. Ask them to identify phrases which mean: *Can I have your name? Can you wait? My name is ...*

> **1** b   **2** c   **3** d   **4** e   **5** a

3 Play the tape again to check.

Language Note
Give students two or three minutes to read this. Point out how *Are you ...? / I'm ...* becomes *Is that ...? / This is ...* on the telephone.

D

1 Ask students to do this exercise orally, with reference to the Language Note. Elicit sentences for the first two prompts from the whole class, then let them continue the dialogue in pairs. When they have finished, ask one pair to perform the dialogue twice in front of the class, the first time without stopping, and the second time, pausing after each sentence to allow any comments or alternative suggestions from the rest of the class.

2 The aim of this activity is to give more oral practice of the same dialogue, having corrected students' first version. Ask two students to model the first four sentences before letting everybody work in pairs.

E [24]

The linking of words in rapid speech is one of the major barriers to comprehension of spoken English. The aim here is to sensitize students to the problem and to give them practice in reproducing correctly linked words in sentences.

Start by writing the two examples on the board, but without the links between words. Say the sentences first with pauses between all the words, so that it sounds 'robotic'. Then say them again, with the correct linking. Elicit which version sounds correct, and why. Ask them to repeat the phrases after you. Then refer them to the rule for linking words in the rubric. Let students work in pairs to marked the linked words; encourage them to say the sentences when they have finished marking them.

> **1** Could I have your name?
> **2** Can I leave a message?
> **3** Hold on a moment.
> **4** Could you ask Ellen to call me back?
> **5** I'm afraid she's not in the office at the moment.

F

As an introduction, ask students if any of them have visited France. Ask which parts of France tourists go to, and what they go to see. This will allow you to elicit / teach some of the key vocabulary from the reading text: *vineyard, wine-tasting, châteaux* (castles).

1 Ask students to read the text individually and then discuss the different activities with a partner. Feed back with the whole class.

> see an exhibition of models of da Vinci's machines; go sightseeing in a balloon; do a car rally; visit châteaux and vineyards in a classic Cadillac; drink champagne

2 Demonstrate by saying what you would like to do, and why. Then let students do the activity in pairs. Ask individual students to report on what their partners would (or wouldn't) like to do, with their reasons.

G [25]

1 Play the tape twice if necessary, allowing students to compare answers after the first listening.

> **1** c
> **2** He has a flight to England on Friday.
> **3** have dinner in a chateau; wine-tasting; ballooning

2 Play the tape again, pausing after each response. Ask students which words David puts particular stress on.

> **1** very kind of you; afraid
> **2** would; nice
> **3** I'd love to

H

Students work in pairs on their list of things to do. If you have students from different regions or countries, pair each person with a partner from the same place.

When they are ready, model the beginning of the dialogue with a stronger student, with you playing the role of the host. Start by saying: *Is that* (student's name)? *Hello, I'm calling about this weekend. Would you like to …?*

Then form new pairs, so students are not with someone from their own country or region (if possible) and ask them to perform the dialogue twice, both as the host and the guest. Monitor, asking students to self-correct any errors you hear.

Optional extra activity
Students could write an e-mail or fax to a friend / business colleague, inviting them to a social occasion: a meal, the theatre, etc. As well as issuing the invitation they need to describe the place and give directions.

3.3 Eating out

A

As a warmer, ask students to write the name of a type of food (e.g. pizza) and the country it comes from. They should then say the name of the food to a partner, who must say the country. With a stronger group, you could start by discussing any of these subjects: favourite foreign food; how often they eat in restaurants; best restaurants in town and why; why fast food restaurants and sandwich bars are so popular.

1 Ask students to look at the menu and ask some initial questions: *What do we call the first / second / third part of a meal? Why is the restaurant called the* Global Village? *Where does the coffee come from?* Then let them work in pairs to identify the countries and make sentences orally, as in the example. Check answers with the whole class. Then deal with any problem vocabulary, e.g. *topped, filled, slices, strips, grated.*

> Nachos – Mexico
> Sushi – Japan
> Onion soup – France
> Paella – Spain
> Lasagne – Italy
> Green curry – Thailand
> Apple strudel – Germany
> Kulfi – India
> Strawberries and cream – Britain

2 Let students work on this in pairs or threes. You could let them use bilingual or picture dictionaries to help them add to the lists. After five minutes, draw up a list on the board from students' suggestions.

> **Possible answers:**
> 1 cucumber, celery, onion
> 2 raspberry, orange, pear
> 3 potatoes, couscous
> 4 butter, milk, yoghurt
> 5 lamb, duck, pork

3 This activity highlights the language used to describe dishes. Refer students back to the menu to find examples of all the terms in the left-hand column, then ask them to complete the task individually before comparing answers with a partner. Check answers.

> 1 menu   4 in lettuce
> 2 coconuts   5 in the oven
> 3 red wine

4 Start by giving an example from your own country. If it's a dish that all students will know, don't give the name, and ask them to guess from your description. Then ask each student to write the names of three dishes. Give them a few minutes to think about the descriptions. You will probably need to help with vocabulary. Put students into pairs and tell them to take it in turns to be the host. If possible, pair together people who are from different countries or regions.

B 26

1 Play the tape twice if necessary, pausing after the first listening to give students time to discuss their answers.

> She chooses onion soup and paella.
> He chooses guacamole and green curry.

2 Let students look at the Language Note, then play the tape once more without stopping, to let students tick the expressions they hear. Then play again, pausing every time you hear one of the expressions, and asking individual students to repeat the whole sentence.

Language Note
Elicit why we would say *some* water, but *a* or *another* glass, to remind them of the countable / uncountable distinction. Remind them of the use of the verb *have* for all eating and drinking activities: *have a drink / breakfast / a meal,* etc. You can also point out the use of *I'll …* for decisions in the expression *I'll have …*

3 Divide the class into threes and let them role-play ordering a meal in a restaurant.

C

1 Do a couple of examples first with the whole class to point out that some answers could be countable or uncountable, e.g. *some / a bottle of water*. Then let them complete the exercise in pairs before checking with you.

> **C:** a jug (of water), a bottle (of wine), a (wine) glass, a serviette, a knife, a fork, a spoon, (a coffee)
> **U:** some butter, (some wine), some bread, some fruit, some salt, (some coffee)

2 Refer students to the first example sentence and ask them if they can see anything strange about it. Point out that normally in questions we use *any*, but here it is different. Refer them to Part 3 of the Language Note on page 39. To check understanding, write the following four sentences on the board and ask them which ones would take *some* and which ones *any* (1, 4: *some*; 2, 3: *any*).

> 1 Would you like _____ coffee?
> 2 Have you got _____ brothers and sisters?
> 3 Are there _____ buses after midnight?
> 4 Could I have _____ fruit, please?

Then let students do the activity in pairs before checking back with you.

D

This exercise presents and practises the language you need at the end of the meal when you are getting the bill, paying, thanking your host, etc.

1 Start by asking three of the stronger students in the class to imagine a dialogue at the end of a meal. One of them is the host, another the guest, and the third the waiter. They've just finished their coffee. Ask them to improvise their conversation in front of the class, with other students offering suggestions when needed. You can supply key words and phrases from the dialogue they are going to hear on the tape, if necessary.

Then ask all students to complete the task individually and compare with a partner. Feed back as a class.

> 1 e   W–H   5 c   G–H
> 2 f / d H–W   6 d / f H–W
> 3 a   H–W   7 b   G–H
> 4 g   G–H

2 Play the tape, without stopping, to check answers. Then play it again, pausing at intervals if necessary. Divide the class into threes, and ask them to role-play the whole dialogue with the help of the cues / questions and responses in **1**. Encourage them to do it a second and third time so they all have a chance to play each role.

With a weaker class, ask them to turn to the tapescript on page 165 and read that aloud first before doing it again with just the cues.

E

This exercise consolidates the vocabulary from the unit. Refer students to the game board. Use a coin to illustrate the concept of *heads* and *tails*, then ask one student to throw the coin. Wherever they land, ask them to improvise the conversation with the student on their left, for the benefit of the whole class. Some conversations are longer than others, but each student in the group must speak at least once for every square.

Divide the class into threes and let them play the game. Monitor, asking students to self-correct or correct each other whenever they hear a mistake. Make a note of any conversations that were not done particularly well. When everybody has finished, choose different pairs of students to perform the more problematic dialogues in front of the class. Deal with any linguistic problems that come up.

Optional extra activity
Divide the class into groups of three. Ask them to role-play a whole conversation between waiter, host, and guest, from arrival in the restaurant to payment of the bill and departure. You can use the *Global Village* menu as your 'prop'. You can play the role of waiter / waitress, circulating between the different tables.

Photocopiable activity (page 69)
This gives further practice in telephoning language. Photocopy one sheet for each pair of students, then cut up and divide the 24 cards into two piles for the caller and person receiving the call. Students should not show their cards to their partner. Explain that they are going to make different telephone conversations.

The caller then chooses a card to begin the conversation. He / she says the sentence aloud, laying the card down on the table (face down or face up, depending on how strong the group is). The person called then does the same, choosing a suitable response from his / her cards. Students then continue to lay down in turn until the conversation reaches a natural conclusion. They then shuffle the cards and start again. You may wish to switch roles at this point.

As a follow-up, see which pair can make the longest conversation. Students lay the cards face up on the table in correct order so that you can see if the different exchanges are appropriate. After this, ask them to cover the 'person called' cards and to repeat from memory. Then do the same for the 'caller' cards.

Unit 4 | Visiting a company

4.1 Meeting people

A

This exercise introduces the simple past form of *be*. Refer students to the initial rubric and make sure they understand the situation. Check comprehension of *yesterday evening*. Play the tape once. Check answers, then let students practise the questions and answer in pairs.

> 1 He was in a restaurant with a client.
> 2 She was at a friend's house.
> 3 They were at the cinema.

B

Time expressions often confuse students. This exercise helps them to focus on past time and acts as a lead-in to work on the simple past.

① Ask students to work in pairs, and give them one minute to do the task. Draw a time line on the board and ask the class to help you fill it in. Some students may be unsure where to place *on Tuesday* on the time line. It suggests Tuesday of this week and before yesterday.

> In 1984 – last week – on Tuesday – yesterday morning – at 9 o'clock last night – at 6 o'clock this morning – NOW

② Ask students to fill in a time line for themselves. Go through the model questions and answers, and practise orally. Then let students work in pairs to ask and answer about their time lines. More adventurous ones will try and use other verbs apart from *be*. Others will simply use the model. Either is fine.

C 29

This exercise introduces weak forms of *was* and *were*. The three dialogues offer examples of both strong and weak forms. Where the important information or emphasis is elsewhere in the sentence, the form is weak.

Play the tape for students to do the task. Check answers, then play the tape again for students to repeat. Make sure they can distinguish the strong and weak forms of *was* and *were*. If the verb is the last word in the sentence it should be stressed. If it is the first word it is sometimes stressed. Otherwise it is only stressed to particularly emphasize it.

Language Note
Read through with students. Highlight the contracted forms of *be*. Check they can form the simple past tense of regular verbs by eliciting further example sentences.

D 30

This exercise introduces *yes / no* questions and regular verbs in the simple past tense. The listening has examples of the three pronunciations of *-ed*: /ɪd/, /t/, and /d/.

① Ask students to read the rubric and check comprehension of the questions. Play the tape once for students to complete the task.

② Ask students to listen again to check and to write down the full answers. These all contain regular verbs in the simple past form.

> 1 ✓: Yes I did – and I improved my Spanish too!
> 2 ✓: Yes, I did to start with. I attended classes for two weeks. After that I learned Spanish from my friends.
> 3 ✗: No, I didn't do any sport, but I started to learn the tango.
> 4 ✗: No, I didn't. I lived in a flat in the city.
> 5 ✓: Yes, I did – I really liked the people.
> 6 ✗: Er, no. I failed my statistics exam the first time. But I passed it the second time.

③ Students work in pairs and ask and answer questions about a course they did. Feed back as a class.

④ Play the sentences in ① again and ask students to put the verbs in the answers in the correct columns. Check answers and ask them to add two more verbs to each column.

/t/	/d/	/ɪd/
liked	improved	attended
passed	learned	started
	lived	
	failed	

E

This exercise is a controlled practice of *Wh-* questions. Student A is checking Student B's expenses claim.

Student B has legitimate expenses but has a tendency to overspend. Divide the class into two halves to prepare the Student A and B roles. Let them work with a partner to prepare questions / answers before they form A / B pairs to complete the activity. Student B should not divulge all his information but give answers that his boss is likely to accept, e.g.

- *How did you travel from Birmingham to Manchester?*
  I travelled by taxi.
- *Where did you stay in Liverpool?*
  I stayed at the Royal Hotel.
- *Who did you telephone?*
  I telephoned a contact.
- *Where were you on Wednesday?*
  I worked at home.
- *Who did you visit on Thursday?*
  I visited a customer in Scotland.
- *Who did you play golf with?*
  I played with another important (future) customer.

F 31

This exercise focuses on the language used when welcoming a visitor.

1 Introduce the situation, explaining that the two men have never met and that Yuji is visiting Paco in Madrid. Let students work in pairs to reorder the dialogue. Ask one of the pairs to act out their conversation and see if the rest of the class are in agreement.

2 Play the tape for students to listen and check.

1 i	3 k	5 h	7 d	9 j	11 b
2 a	4 c	6 e	8 f	10 g	

3 Students practise the dialogue in pairs: one student is Yuji and the other himself or herself. Any creativity in the dialogue is to be encouraged.

G 32

This exercise focuses on small talk and begins with a listen and respond activity.

1 Students do not need to open their books. Explain the situation, then play the tape and ask them to jot down a response to the ten prompts. Pool results and listen again if necessary. There will be more than one correct answer. The important point is to understand the questions and reply in a positive, communicative way.

2 Ask students to open their books and match the responses to the prompts they heard on the tape.

1 e	3 j	5 g	7 h	9 d
2 c	4 a	6 b	8 f	10 i

H

1 This activity revises the language of the section. Give students time to look at the prompts before they work in pairs to have a conversation. One possible dialogue would be:

A: *Welcome to New York.*
B: *Thanks very much.*
A: *My name is Martin Jenkins.*
B: *Pleased to meet you Mr Jenkins. I'm John Marshall.*
A: *How was your flight?*
B: *I'm afraid it was late.*
A: *Oh I'm sorry about that. How's the hotel?*
B: *Very nice.*
A: *Would you like anything to drink?*
B: *Could I have an iced tea?*
A: *Certainly. Is this your first trip to the Big Apple?*
B: *Yes, it is.*

2 Students change roles. Encourage them to continue the conversation.

4.2 Reporting on a trip

A

This exercise revises days of the week, times, dates, and numbers, and should be done quickly but carefully. Set a two-minute time limit and monitor carefully. Feed back with the whole class and correct any frequent errors, particularly in days and dates.

B

This exercise practises irregular verbs in the simple past form.

1 Introduce the situation by asking some general questions:

- *Whose diary is it?*
- *Who does she work for?*
- *When was this week?*
- *Where did she go?*

Having established the situation, ask students to work in pairs to complete the gaps in the diary. All the answers can be found in the documents.

1 217	3 Madison	5 Theatre
2 15.20	4 Citronelle	6 The White House

Add follow-up questions as you feed back, e.g. *What play did she see? How much was the taxi?* etc.

2 In this activity there are both regular and irregular verbs. It can be done with the whole class or in pairs.

They are all *Wh-* questions so the voice should go down at the end of the question not up. At the end of the activity, ask students to invent three more questions each (based on Piera's diary), to ask their partners.

> 1 She flew to Washington.
> 2 She left London at 12.15.
> 3 She took a taxi.
> 4 She stayed at the Madison Hotel.
> 5 She visited the Training Centre.
> 6 She had lunch at Citronelle.
> 7 She went to Baltimore.
> 8 She flew.
> 9 She returned to Italy.
> 10 She wrote it on Sunday.

3 We now concentrate on question formation. The answer is supplied so the exercise is purely mechanical. Write the table below on the board so students can see the formation. Highlight the inversion of auxiliary and subject, and the infinitive form of the verb. Write in other words as students supply the questions.

Question word / phrase	auxiliary	subject	verb
Where	did	she	go …?
Who			have dinner with?

> 1 What did she do on Wednesday morning?
> 2 Which airline did she fly with?
> 3 Who did she meet on Wednesday evening?
> 4 What time did she have lunch with Priscilla Weiner?
> 5 When did she go / fly to Baltimore?
> 6 Why did she go / fly to Baltimore?
> 7 Where did she have dinner with Sally and Harry?
> 8 Did she visit the White House?

C 33

The class now know a lot about Piera and her trip to the US. This listening exercise revises the verbs and reinforces the structure.

1 Ask students to look at the answers provided. In English we tend to use the same verb in the answer as in the question, so the questions are fairly easy to guess.

2 Play the tape once and check answers. Ask students to repeat the dialogue in short chunks.

> 1 How are you?
> 2 When did you get back from Washington?
> 3 How was the meeting at Citibank?
> 4 Did you go out in the evening?
> 5 Where did you stay?
> 6 Did you go shopping?
> 7 What did you do yesterday?

Language Note
Read through with students. Refer them to the Language File on page 157 for a full list of irregular verbs.

Optional extra activity
To consolidate the use of regular / irregular verbs in the past tense, ask students to work in pairs and devise a quiz of at least ten questions about famous people or events in the past, e.g. *When did the first man walk on the moon?* When they have finished, ask them to give their quiz to another pair to complete. Full answers should be given.

D

This exercise provides a model for writing an e-mail of thanks.

1 Ask students to work in pairs to put the e-mail in order. Point out that an e-mail is more like an oral message than a written one and that an e-mail message can be quite informal if you know the person you are e-mailing.

> Dear Isaac
> Many thanks for your warm welcome in Washington.
> I had a very good three days and I think the meetings were useful.
> I also enjoyed the meals and the trip to the theatre.
> When you come to Italy next month do not hesitate to contact me.
> Thanks again.
> Kindest Regards
> Piera

2 Students can now write their own e-mail of thanks, using the model.

> **Model answer:**
> Dear Lorraine,
> Many thanks for your warm welcome in LA.
> I had a good trip and I think the conference was useful.
> I also enjoyed the day-trip to San Francisco and the barbecue at your house.
> When you come here in August do not hesitate to contact me.
> Thanks again
> Kindest Regards

E

This exercise introduces students to word collocations. Learning them can increase students' active vocabulary and also make them sound more English.

1 Ask students to match the words individually, then compare answers in pairs before checking back with you.

```
send an e-mail
take a train
write a report
make a phone-call
go on a trip
meet a customer
attend a meeting
```

2 Let students work in pairs to invent sentences using the collocations. Check they have used the correct form of the verb.

F

This speaking exercise practises making and answering questions, using the simple past.

1 Divide the class into A / B pairs and refer them to the relevant information. Each student has a diary and they should complete their partner's diary by asking questions about each day. With weaker students, you may wish to begin by asking them to complete the diary on page 49 with their own schedule first; this will highlight the information they need to ask for.

2 Students will discover that they nearly met last week because they were both interviewed for the same job. Student A was lucky enough to get the job!

4.3 Describing company structure

A [34]

This exercise focuses on the language for introducing people and the jobs they do.

1 There are four dialogues. Ensure students understand the situation. Play the tape once and collate the replies. When you have all the correct answers, listen to the dialogues again, asking students to repeat each line. Finally, ask students to act out the dialogues.

```
a  Accountant
b  Marketing Director
c  in charge of Human Resources
d  Company Lawyer
e  Sales Director
f  Personal Assistant
g  Head of Research
```

2 This activity revises the language of introductions. Let students introduce themselves to the person on their right. Then ask them to introduce themselves and their partner to other people in the room, using expressions from the dialogues such as: *I'd like you to meet ... Do you know ...? Let me introduce you to ..., This is ...*

B

This exercise continues the theme of jobs. Let students work in pairs to match the jobs to the descriptions. As a follow-up, ask if these jobs exist in their company and in what numbers. Point out that several of these titles vary from company to company: *training officer* might be a whole job in one company or part of a person's job in another. Words like *director, manager, officer* are fairly interchangeable these days.

```
1  training officer
2  laboratory technician
3  managing director
4  quality control manager
5  sales representative
6  personal assistant
7  purchasing manager
```

C

This exercise introduces new vocabulary and revises other words connected with company structure.

1 As a warmer, talk about water and whether the class drink tap water or bottled water. Ask them which brands are famous in their countries and whether there is a lot of advertising by water companies. Ask them to read the text individually and complete the gaps, using the words in the box.

1 subsidiary	5 production sites	9 takeover
2 customers	6 research centre	10 turnover
3 division	7 product	11 market leader
4 brands	8 acquisition	12 market share

2 Draw the chart on the board and ask students to complete it.

Teacher's Book 25

> 1 parent company 4 CEO
> 2 subsidiary 5 research centres
> 3 brands

3 This should be a straightforward task for those in work. For those who are yet to work, try and access Internet sites where this information is readily available.

D

This exercise focuses on the different departments within a company.

1 Ask students to look at the document extracts and suggest what they are: a letter of application, a bank statement, a spreadsheet, a chart, a message, a contract. Let them work individually to do the matching, then compare in pairs before checking back with you.

> 1 d   2 f   3 c   4 e   5 a   6 b

2 As a class, make a list of other departments in a company, e.g. Production, Customer Services or Aftersales, General Services, Logistics, Transport, Packaging, Planning.

3 Ask students to work through the exercise individually, then check answers with the whole class.

> 1 Finance
> 2 in the Research and Development department
> 3 Sales people work in the Sales and Marketing department.
> 4 Lawyers work in the Legal department.
> 5 PR people work in the Communications department.
> 6 Training Managers work in the Human Resources department.

E `35a`

This exercise contextualizes the vocabulary from previous exercises in the section and introduces vocabulary describing offices and equipment. By the end of the section, the class will be able to make a short presentation about their department, as they would need to do if they were receiving visitors.

1 Set the scene and check students understand the situation. Play `35a` twice as they need to note a lot of information. Collate the information on the board.

> 1 **Research:** 14 (4 + 10); well-equipped laboratory and offices; software research; not in main building, lot of budget spent on travel
> 2 **Purchasing:** 12 (5 + 7); large open-plan office on second floor plus two on top floor; purchasing raw material, components, supplies; lot of travel to China, Philippines, and Korea; use fax and e-mail a lot
> 3 **Human Resources:** 7 (6 + 1); first floor of main building; recruitment and training; lot of budget spent on computer and language training
> 4 **Communications:** 3; large open-plan office – ground floor; internal and external communications and public relations; main projects are company newsletter and annual report

2 This activity takes an extract from each department. Play `35b` Students need to listen carefully and complete the sentences.

> 1 work ... lot ... computer ... spend ... budget ... travel
> 2 ... responsible ... all ... supplies
> 3 There are ... of us
> 4 in charge of

Language Note
Read through with students. The language will be useful in .

F

This exercise allows the students to make a short presentation of their department in a non-technical way. The talk should cover the personnel of the department, facilities and equipment, and activity. Ask students to prepare their presentation as a homework task and then listen to them in class at a later date.

Photocopiable activity (page 70)
This provides further practice in exchanging information about companies. Each student should have a grid with complete information for one company. Working in fours, they should ask and answer questions to complete the information about the other three companies.

Alternatively, to make a longer activity, cut up all the information into cards and ask students to work in small groups to reassemble it.

Unit 5 | New developments

5.1 Current activities

A

First, write the following on the board and ask students to match the phrases on the left with the appropriate time expression. Establish that the present continuous is used for present actions in progress at the time of speaking.

He stays at the Ritz Hotel ...	last week.
He's staying at the Ritz Hotel ...	every year.
He stayed at the Ritz Hotel ...	at the moment.

1 Ask students to complete the task individually. Let them compare answers in pairs before checking back with you.

| 1 are building | 3 is training | 5 are assembling |
| 2 are doing | 4 is designing | |

2 Answer these questions as a whole-class activity.

3 Elicit one or two examples, then let students do the task in pairs. Monitor for correct use of the present continuous. Ask individual students to report back on their partners' present projects.

Language Note
Point out that the present continuous isn't only used for actions happening at this very moment; it can also be used with other time expressions which indicate a longer period of time such as *today, this week, this month, this year*, etc.

B

1 Let students complete these two tasks in pairs before checking back with you.

1	1 d	2 e	3 a	4 b	5 c
2	1 introduce	2 improve	3 recruit	4 lay off
	5 look for			

2 Elicit two or three example questions from the whole class first, and ask individual students to answer them with reference to their own company. Then let them continue the activity in pairs. Monitor for correct use of the present continuous in both questions and answers.

Language Note
When students have read this, write three other verbs on the board, e.g. *work, buy, travel*. Elicit some more pairs of sentences where the verb is used first in the present simple, then in the present continuous form, e.g. *He works for IBM. He's working in the head office this month.*

C 36

This exercise gives practice in distinguishing between the present simple and present continuous. Start by asking students to give the names and nationalities of any oil companies they know. Elicit / teach the products such companies typically sell: petrol – leaded / unleaded / diesel; oil; gas; heating fuel, etc.

1 Give students time to read the questions, and deal with any queries. Then play the tape once or twice as necessary, giving them time to compare answers in pairs before checking back with you.

| 1 Oil and petrol. |
| 2 Training. |
| 3 It's building a big technology centre. |
| 4 Argentina. |
| 5 Because it's introducing a lot of new technology and computer tools. |

2 Point out that some of the sentences and questions are in the present simple and others in the present continuous. Let students complete the task orally in pairs, then play the tape again to check, stopping after each sentence.

> J: Which company are you with?
> A: I work for Repsol YPKT. The company also manufactures and distributes gas and electricity.
> J: What job do you do?
> A: I train new employees. We're investing a lot of money in training at the moment.
> J: Is the company expanding very quickly?
> A: Yes, Repsol YPK is developing its activity in Latin America. In Spain we're building a new technology centre.
> J: Where in Latin America does Repsol operate?
> A: The company has a new headquarters in Buenos Aires.
> J: What are you working on at the moment?
> A: We are organizing specialized training programmes. The company is introducing a lot of new technology.

Teacher's Book 27

D

1 Let students work on this individually. Then ask them to compare answers with a partner before checking back with you.

1 is expanding	5 has	9 is helping
2 owns	6 is selling	10 is sponsoring
3 produces	7 are	11 is researching
4 specializes	8 is growing	

2 Elicit answers to these questions from the whole class.

Optional extra activity
Ask students to describe a foreign company operating in their country (both usual and current activity) but without saying the name. The others must guess what it is. Students could also write a similar description as a homework task.

E 37

Read the initial rubric with students, and point out that the small grammatical words are often unstressed because they are not the most important words in a sentence. Model the sound /ə/ for students, and then the words *for, of, to, and, but, do, does, are* in their weak (unstressed) form.

1 Before listening, ask students to predict what words go in the spaces, then play the tape to check. Play individual sentences again if they are not sure what word they heard.

are; for; does; and; do; of; are; to; from; at

2 Play the tape and ask students to repeat in chorus and / or individually. When trying to produce the correct /ə/ sound, they may have a tendency to stress the unstressed words. If this happens, play the tape again, and ask them to identify the words that really are stressed in each sentence. Then get them to repeat the sentences again. Finally, let them practise the whole dialogue in pairs.

5.2 Company developments

A

This exercise introduces the language for describing trends. Start by asking students what kind of information about companies is given in graphs and diagrams: sales, profits, market share, share prices, etc.

1 Refer students to the bar chart. Check understanding of the different regions by asking them to name three countries in: Europe, Asia-Pacific, Latin America. Then ask a few checking questions about the figures, e.g. *What was the percentage of sales in the USA in 1999?* Ask them to underline all the verbs in the six sentences. Draw three arrows on the board, one pointing up, another down, and the third horizontal. Elicit which verbs go with which arrow. Then let them complete the task individually or in pairs before checking back with you.

1 F (only one)	4 F (rose by 1%)
2 T	5 T
3 F (four regions)	6 F (increased)

2 Let students complete this individually before checking back with you. Explain that more than one answer is possible for some gaps.

1 fell / decreased / went down; fall / go down / decrease
2 remained stable
3 remained stable; went up / increased / rose
4 rose / increased / went up

Language Note
The verbs are given here in the present continuous and past simple forms, as these are the tenses which will be contrasted in the exercise that follows. Check understanding of the difference between *by, from,* and *to* by asking students for two other example sentences based on the Motorola bar chart in **A**.

B

1 Let students complete the task individually (it is not necessary to read the text in detail at this stage). Then check answers, pointing out the conventions for saying different types of numbers.

1 nineteen eighty-four
2 two point five nine
3 twelve per cent
4 seven hundred and twenty-five thousand eight hundred

2 All the numbers are of a similar type to those in the first question. Monitor the pairs, and when you hear a number given incorrectly, refer them back to the written form of the different numbers in **1**, and ask them to correct themselves.

3 Introduce some of the vocabulary from the text by asking students to put the following words in logical order: *retirement, birth, marriage, death, divorce*. Then let them complete the task individually, comparing answers with a partner before checking back with you.

> 1 fell – from
> 2 went up – by
> 3 are deciding
> 4 rose – to
> 5 is also falling
> 6 is increasing
> 7 went up – to
> 8 increased – by
> 9 is continuing
> 10 is also falling
> 11 went down – by

4 Let students work in pairs. If possible, put students from different countries together. Point out that they don't have to give figures in each case. When they have finished, ask one pair to report back to the class on the different trends. If your students are from the same country, see if they agree with the analysis given by the pair reporting back. If they are from different countries, compare and contrast the students' reports. You may like to build up a table on the board, with one row for each trend discussed and a column for each country represented. In each box, put an upward, downward, or horizontal arrow to represent the trend, based on students' views.

Optional extra activity
If you feel it is appropriate, ask students to research some figures for one of the trends in **4** and to compile the information in the form of a bar chart. Students can present their information to the class in the next lesson.

C

This exercise gives further practice in describing trends. Divide the class into A / B pairs and refer them to the relevant file. Point out that they have one completed graph – this is the one they will describe to their partner, who will draw it. The other blank grid is for drawing their partner's graph. When they have finished drawing, they must guess what their partner's company sells. Monitor and make sure they are using the correct language: *increase / decrease*, etc.

When they have finished, ask them how they knew that the companies sold skis (Student A) and children's toys (Student B), e.g. sales in Student A's company rose to more than £50,000 in the winter, but decreased for the rest of the year. You may like to teach the term *reach a peak*.

D [38]

1 Introduce the subject by asking how many students have an Internet connection. Ask them to make a list of different uses of the Internet, and pool ideas on the board.

Then refer students to the table and pie chart and ask them what they represent. Check they understand what *e-commerce* means (shopping by Internet). Ask a few comprehension questions, e.g. *How many Internet users were there in the USA in 1997? In the Asia-Pacific market, how many families in developing countries had an Internet connection in 1997?* Alternatively, say some of the numbers from the diagrams, and ask students to say what they refer to.

Then answer the questions as a whole-class activity.

> The first is a table; the second is a pie chart.
> There are segments and figures on the pie chart; and columns and figures on the table.

2 Start by asking students what information is missing from the diagrams. Then play the tape twice, allowing students time to compare notes each time before checking back with you. Ask them if there's anything that surprises them about the figures.

> 1 878%
> 2 $34.5 bn
> 3 $26 bn
> 4 7%
> 5 28%

3 Play the tape again, stopping at the end of each target sentence to allow students to write the missing words. Replay sentences as necessary. Do a whole-class feedback at the end.

> 1 have a look at; see
> 2 Notice that
> 3 draw your attention
> 4 as you can see

Language Note
The Language Note highlights the language used in [38] to refer to visual aids. Ensure that students understand the vocabulary and practise saying the sentences.

E [39]

1 Play the tape for students to complete the task individually.

2 Play the tape again to check and ask students to repeat the words in chorus and / or individually.

> ●○   figures   segment   column
> ○●   remain   Japan   compare
> ●○○   India   period   diagram
> ○●○   recruitment   consumer   percentage

5.3 Personal developments

A [40]

Start by briefly revising the language of introductions (first seen in Unit 1). Ask three students to come to the front of the class. A and B are colleagues, C is a visitor who has just arrived in the company. A and B have never met C. Ask them to improvise a dialogue. Stop the conversation if they say anything inappropriate and ask the rest of the class for suggestions. Then choose another three students. This time they are all colleagues returning after two weeks' holiday. Repeat the same process as for the first conversation.

1 Let students do the task individually, and then compare answers in pairs before checking back with you.

> **1** c **2** a **3** d **4** e **5** b

2 Do this as a whole-class activity.

> first time meeting: 1, 4 (5)
> when you know the person: 2, 3, 5

3 Ask students to say in which pair of photos the conversation seems more formal, and in which more relaxed. Then play the tape for students to match the conversations to the pictures. What do they think is the relationship between the speakers? How did they arrive at that conclusion?

> **1** Conversation 1: photo A
> Conversation 2: photo B
> Conversation 1: boss and employee
> Conversation 2: two friends

Refer students to the second question and elicit answers. Play the tape again to check, pausing when you hear examples of the different conversation features, and asking students what the speaker has just said.

> **2** aB   bA   cA   dB   eA   fB

4 Refer students to the Language Note. Point out that *How are things?* is a more informal way of saying *How are you?*, and that *pretty good* means the same as *quite good*. Then play the tape again for students to note the expressions used. Let them compare answers in pairs before checking back with you.

> Expressions used: *How are you? Very well, thank you. I'm pleased to hear that. How are things? Sorry to hear that. How's the family? Really? That's incredible! That's great news! I'm happy to hear that.*

B

This exercise gives practice in using the expressions learned in **A**.

1 Let students complete this individually, then compare answers with a partner. Tell them to go straight on to the next task.

> **1** a, b   **2** b, c   **3** a, b   **4** b, c   **5** a, b   **6** a, b

2 Let students complete this in pairs. Check the questions for **1** and **2** with the whole class. When they are saying the questions, encourage them to sound enthusiastic and interested, rather than using 'flat' intonation.

> **Possible answers:**
> 1 How's your husband / partner?
> 2 How's business? / How are things?
> 3 How's your daughter?
> 4 How's your job?
> 5 This could be any question using *how*.

3 Elicit some example questions from the whole class for each of the topics, then let students do the activity in pairs. Monitor, and intervene where responses are not forthcoming or don't sound interested enough. At the end, ask one pair to perform their dialogue in front of the class, and use it as a basis for correction.

C [41]

1 Read the rubric with students, and ask them what questions they think Danuta's colleague will ask. Play the tape once, and give them a minute or two to discuss their answers to the first question before checking back with you. Ask them what evidence there is that the trip was a positive experience.

> Her trip was generally positive. Accept any reasonable answers based on the tapescript.

2 Play the tape again. Stop when you hear the first question – students may need to listen again, as the structure is new to them. Then play the rest of the tape. Check answers with the whole class. Point out that the structure *What is / was ... like?* is similar in meaning to *How is / was ...?*, but that the first is more common. Let them read the Language Note that follows.

> **A**
> What was New York like?
> What was your hotel like?
> How was the conference?
> What were the presentations like?

3 Give students time to write any information they remember in column B, then play the tape again to check. Let them compare answers before checking back with you. As an introduction to the vocabulary section that follows, ask them to think of adjectives that mean the opposite of those given in Danuta's answers: *noisy – quiet, exciting – dull*, etc.

> **B**
> noisy, but exciting
> small room, but hotel very clean
> friendly people, made some useful contacts
> a little boring

D

1 Let students do this in pairs before checking back with you.

> 1 i   2 f   3 c   4 g   5 e   6 h   7 j   8 d
> 9 a   10 b
>
> **Positive:** quiet, friendly, clean, convenient, useful, interesting, fantastic
> **Negative:** noisy, unfriendly, expensive, dirty, inconvenient, useless, boring, terrible
> **Could be negative or positive depending on context:** small, large, long, short, cheap

2 Look at the example for *towns* with the whole class, then check understanding by doing the second item, *the weather*, together. Let students complete the other items in pairs before checking back with you.

A	B	C
Towns	easy	large / quiet / modern
The weather	friendly	cold / wet / dry / sunny
People	inconvenient	unfriendly / small / noisy / interesting
Hotels	difficult	inconvenient / fantastic / expensive / cheap / quiet
Meetings/trips	clean	interesting / useless / useful / exciting / short
Presentations	large	useless / long / fantastic / boring / interesting

Optional extra activity
Ask students to play a guessing game in groups of three or four. One student makes a sentence with one of the words in it, and the others must guess what it is, e.g. *This hotel is very ... because it's on a main road.*

E

This exercise practises *What was ... like?* and allows students to use the descriptive vocabulary in context. Divide the class into A / B pairs and refer them to the relevant information. Make sure they understand the situation, and elicit possible questions for the different subjects: journey, hotel, meetings, etc. Then let them work in their pairs, making sure that they note down the answers to their questions. When they have finished, form new A / A and B / B pairs, and ask them to compare the notes they made about their partner's trip.

F

1 Let students do this individually, then compare answers before checking back with you.

> 1 d   2 e   3 a   4 f   5 b   6 c

2 Let students do this in pairs, then discuss possible answers with the whole class. Discuss also how you might respond to the different expressions, e.g. *Have a good weekend. Thanks. You too.*

> 1 Did you have a good weekend / a nice meal / a good trip?
> 2 Bottoms up.
> 4 I hope it goes well.
> 5 Have a good weekend / a nice holiday.
> 6 Speak to you tomorrow / next week / later.

Photocopiable activity (page 71)
This provides additional material for practising presentations. Divide students into groups of three. Give each student one of the graphs. Give them five minutes to prepare a presentation, which they should then present to their two colleagues.

Unit 6 | Arrangements

6.1 Dates and schedules

A `42`

As this section deals with a lot of times and dates, it is a good idea to begin with a revision warmer based on them. In a large class you can ask everybody to write down a favourite date, and then ask students to change seats until they are chronologically placed. In a smaller class ask them to write down the dates of birthdays in their immediate family, and then collate them chronologically on the board. To practise times, prepare some cards with times written on them – some in words and some in numbers. Students should read out the time on the card to the rest of the class, who write it down. When they have written down ten different times, they should put them in chronological order. Collate them on the board and check pronunciation. Remind students of the difference between *a.m.* and *p.m.*

Ask students to read the rubric and look at the conference programme. Ask some general comprehension questions:

– What is the conference about?
– What is the conference location?
– How long is the conference?
– Who are the organizers?
– Is the programme complete?

Then ask the class what information is missing – the hand-written notes represent things they need to find out. Play the tape once.

> **Guest Speaker:** Elizabeth Cortes
> **Arriving from:** Boston
> **Arrival time:** midday on Wednesday
> **Hotel:** Ramada
> **Nights:** one
> **Room:** double
> **Professor Lingwood – start time:** 2.30
> **Subject:** T E R N
> Professor Denier is not coming.

Collate the answers on the board, replaying the tape if necessary. Focus on the language the speakers use to ask for / give the information, e.g. *When is she arriving? She's flying in from Boston on Wednesday morning.* All the sentences use the present continuous to describe a future planned action. The idea of using a present tense to describe future time is difficult for many students to grasp so take your time and let them see / listen to lots of examples. Refer them to the Language Note.

B

Now that you have presented the concept and looked at the language, it is time to practise the form. In this exercise students have to make questions for the answers provided. A number of the questions appeared in **A**. Collate the answers on the board.

Highlight the inversion of auxiliary and subject and the position of the preposition at the end of the sentence. It is also perfectly acceptable to put the preposition at the end rather than the beginning of the question.

> 1 When is Elizabeth Cortes arriving?
> 2 Where is she arriving from?
> 3 What time is she arriving?
> 4 Who is she coming with?
> 5 Where are they staying?
> 6 How long are they staying?
> 7 What is she speaking about?

C

This exercise continues the controlled practice of the present continuous. Divide the class into A / B pairs and refer them to the relevant information. Each student is arranging the arrivals and transfers for the conference but has five pieces of information missing. Their partner has this information. By using *How long ...?, Where ...? When ...?* questions they can complete the information. Feed back as a class.

D `43a`

① Give students two minutes to read the fax. They should read the conference programme in **A** as well, to see how Jaime Gallado's plans fit in with it. With a weaker class you can ask some comprehension questions, e.g. *When is he going to Rio? When is he speaking?*

32 Teacher's Book

2 Play `43a` once and ask students to write down their replies. Communicative response is more important than accuracy in this exercise, although the ideal would be a combination of both.

> **Possible answers:**
> 1 Speaking.
> 2 Yes, I am.
> 3 I'm going on the 26th July.
> 4 Four nights.
> 5 At the Sheraton.
> 6 Yes, on the Friday morning.
> 7 Underground Train Systems in the 21st century.
> 8 No, I'm not free.
> 9 I'm meeting Thérèse Blanc.

3 Play `43b` once and check answers. Compare students' suggestions with the answers on the tape. If they give the correct information or response then that is fine.

E `44a`

1 This exercise focuses on ordinal numbers in dates. Play `44a` once and ask students to circle the ordinal number they hear.

2 Play the tape again and check answers. Ask students to say the numbers aloud including those not on the tape.

> 60th 12th 18th 3rd 20th 31st 13th 15th

3 Ask students to complete the sentences individually and play `44b` to check. Students should then practise reading the sentences aloud.

> 1 fifth   2 eighth   3 thirtieth   4 first   5 fourth

Language Note
This clarifies the differences in dates in British and American English. Point out that with the development of global networks American usage is becoming more common in other countries.

F

1 This is a similar exercise to the warmer suggested in **A**. It is a combination of language and logic. The order is shown on the right in the answer box below.

11/09/99 (UK)	4
11/23/89 (USA)	1
22 September 1998	3
twenty-first of September nineteen ninety-eight	2
9/08/00 (USA)	7
Christmas Day 2000	9
21/12/99 (UK)	6
23 September 1999	5
01/01/01	10
10/10/00	8

2 Ask students to read the dates aloud, chorally and / or individually.

3 A simple pair-work activity where the emphasis should be on saying and understanding dates.

G `45`

1 Ask students to cover up the headlines at the bottom of the page and to guess why the dates are important.

2 Now ask students to uncover the headlines and match them to the dates. Then play the tape to check answers. Ask students to repeat the dates as said on the tape.

> a 1st January 2000
> b 15th April 1912
> c 21st May 1932
> d 11th November 1918
> e 1st June 1953
> f 12th July 1998

3 Elicit the months missing from the list in **1**, then let students work in pairs to complete the task. Feed back as a class.

Optional extra activity
Ask students to work in pairs. Tell them to get out their diaries and to ask each other questions about what they are doing on certain dates, e.g. *What are you doing on 5th April?* Feed back as a class.

6.2 Getting connected

This section deals with telephone language, taking and leaving messages, and other problems that can occur on the phone

A `46`

As a warmer, ask students if they ever make / receive phone calls in English and, if so, what problems they have. Try and get them to be specific about the problems. They might offer the following:
- Making calls: the person is out / difficult to leave a message; difficulty in understanding because of speed or bad line; difficulty in understanding because there is no body language to help

– Receiving calls: strong accents of speakers or people speaking too fast; taking messages – spelling numbers; surprise – a call can come in at any time

The section will help them with these problems.

1 Check students understand that Jordi is trying to contact Diana. Play the tape once and elicit the four problems he encounters.

> 1 The line is busy.
> 2 There is no reply from her office.
> 3 She is out.
> 4 He's got the wrong extension.

2 Play the tape again to listen for more detailed information.

> 1 HK Oil & Gas
> 2 04345-4631
> 3 Sales
> 4 tomorrow
> 5 Friday
> 6 663-4562

3 This activity focuses on particular expressions used on the phone. Ask students to work out which dialogues the expressions come from. Play each dialogue again, one at a time, and ask them to listen and repeat. The dialogues are short enough to act out. For extra dramatic effect and authenticity, have students sitting back to back.

> | a 4 | c 2 | e 1 | g 3 | i 2 | k 4 |
> | b 1/2 | d 4 | f 4 | h 1 | j 3 | l 3 |

B

This exercise helps to reinforce the pairing of certain expressions used on the telephone. Some are answers to questions and others are responses to statements. Let students work in pairs to match the expressions. When reporting back, ask a student from one pair to read out a sentence from 1–9, and a student from another pair to read out a response from a–i. The expressions should sound natural.

> | 1 f | 3 i | 5 a | 7 d | 9 h |
> | 2 g | 4 c | 6 e | 8 b | |

C

This exercise allows students to choose and improvise the language required to handle a complex telephone call. Let students work in pairs to plan their dialogue. Monitor and help where appropriate. One person should be making the call and one receiving. Strong pairs can reverse the roles and start again. When they are well rehearsed, ask one or two pairs to act out their dialogues. Students can write out their dialogues as a homework task.

D 47

One of the problems encountered on the phone is the pace people speak at. Contracted forms seem to add pace to utterances. This exercise is designed to increase students' awareness of contracted forms from a listening perspective, and to help them to use them when speaking.

1 Ask students which words are likely to be contracted in the sentences.

2 Play the tape to check and ask students to repeat the sentences.

> | 1 I'm | 4 You're ... | 7 He's ... |
> | 2 Where's ... | 5 ... I'll ... | 8 He's ... |
> | 3 When's ... | 6 I'm ... she's ... | |

E 48

This exercise focuses on taking messages. Explain the situation and check students understand the rubric. Play the tape once, pausing after each message. Collate information on the board and play the tape again to complete the missing information. If students have their own tape, this exercise could be done for homework, where they can listen at their own pace.

> 1 27th May, 3 p.m. James Lee. Call back this afternoon on 452-98577.
> 2 Patricia Lopez. Dinner cancelled on 9th June. Going to Australia.
> 3 May 26th, 7.30 p.m. Suntours travel agent called. Ticket ready for Manila. Will post tomorrow.
> 4 Jordi Marrero called. Staying at Royal Garden Hotel. Call before 9 p.m., Friday May 27th. His number is 453-49823.

F

1 In groups of three, students make dialogues by choosing one expression from each row. The expression they choose should follow logically from the one from the previous row. When they have finished, ask them to act out their dialogues, then form new groups of three to make another dialogue.

2 The final task is to finish the conversation. Jordi has got through to Diana. They now need to confirm the arrangements for dinner.

6.3 Arranging to meet

A

This exercise continues the topic area of dates, times, and appointments.

1 Establish that the time is 7.30 p.m. on April 3rd. Then ask the eight questions in any order as quickly as possible. This gets students to think and react quickly. It does not matter if you repeat questions, the point is to keep the class on their toes.

1 7.00 p.m.	5 Wednesday
2 27th March	6 1st April
3 4th April	7 30th March
4 Sunday	8 Friday

2 Write the table on the board and choose a student as writer. Elicit suggestions and let the writer complete the table. Check understanding by writing the real days of the week next to the time expressions: if today is Monday then yesterday was Sunday, etc. Remind students that days of the week take a capital letter in English.

| −3: three days ago |
| −2: the day before yesterday |
| −1: yesterday |
| 0: today |
| +1: tomorrow |
| +2: the day after tomorrow |
| +3: in three days' time |

3 Ask students to work in pairs. Remind them that it is still 7.30 p.m. on April 3rd. Ask them to look at the diary to establish where that date appears. The diary is for last week and this week. Students work through each sentence and add the information to the diary. Collate the information as a class. Ask them when Natasha has any spare time because she is going to be telephoning to make some appointments.

Monday March 27– Thursday 30:	holiday
Friday March 31:	trade fair in Boston
Saturday April 1:	New York
Sunday April 2:	fly to New Orleans
Tuesday April 4:	9–12 sales meeting
Wednesday April 5:	4.00 p.m. Jack Rogers; 6.00 p.m. Yuki Aoki
Friday April 7:	fly to Washington
Saturday April 8:	friends in Baltimore

B [49]

These dialogues are quite long so you may wish to play them one at a time. Elicit who the appointment is with and when it is fixed for. Write the information on the board and add two more columns for later. After the first listening you will have the following information on the board.

Person	Relationship	Time	Language used
Erika	friend	10.30 p.m. Tuesday	
Mikael Stefansson	formal	7.00 p.m. Wednesday	
Dr Jung	met before	9.00 p.m. tonight	
Ms Aoki	new acquaintance	12.30 p.m. Thursday	

When the answers have been established focus on the language used. Listen again and repeat key expressions, and add them to the board. Point out those which are formal and those which are less formal. Refer students to the Language Note for more information.

C

This exercise provides controlled practice of the language for making arrangements and appointments. Divide the class into A / B pairs and refer them to the relevant information. Using the less formal language in the Language Note, students have to try to arrange a time to meet. They will find that the best place to meet is at the airport at about 7.30 p.m. Monitor and then discuss as a class.

D [50]

This exercise focuses on the language used to change an appointment.

1 Set the scene and remind students that Natasha and Mikael Stefansson do not know each other so the language used is quite formal. Play the tape for students to answer the questions.

| 1 c | 2 b | 3 c | 4 c | 5 a | 6 b |

2 Play the tape again to focus on the actual language used. Ask students to listen and repeat the key expressions, then complete the table. Spend a little time looking at the Language Note, which illustrates the difference between *cancel*, *postpone*, and *bring forward*.

1 Would it be possible to change it?
2 Could we bring it forward a couple of hours?
3 I'm afraid I'm busy.
4 Could we postpone it to Friday?
5 How about another day? Are you free on Thursday?
6 So that's 8 o'clock on the 6th, then.

3 Let students work in pairs on this problem. They need to read very carefully. Feed back with the whole class and show the steps used to calculate the answer on the board.

> Wednesday January 16th at 7.00 p.m.
> brought forward an hour > 6.00 p.m.
> moved to same time following day > January 17th
> postponed for a week > January 24th
> brought forward by two days > January 22nd
> following day one hour later > January 23rd at 7.00 p.m.
> I was an hour late > 8.00 p.m.
> She arrived half an hour later > January 23rd at 8.30 p.m.

4 Divide the class into A / B pairs as in **C**. Ask them to refer back to their files and to rearrange the time of their meeting.

E

This exercise illustrates how e-mails can have a very oral style. Let students work in threes to order the e-mails. As a homework task, ask students to write a similar series of e-mails.

> b, f, d, e, a, h, g, c

Optional extra activity

Ask students to create and act out a phone call from Tina to Heinz, to change their plans the day before her arrival.

Photocopiable activity (page 72)

This provides further practice in telephone language. Ask students to imagine that they have just arrived in the office. The following documents are in their in-tray. Each document requires a telephone response. In pairs, ask students to decide what to do and in what order of priority.

The next stage is to create a telephone dialogue for each document.

Unit 7 | Describing and comparing

7.1 Comparisons and contrasts

A

As a warmer, write the following adjectives on the board.

| fast | easy | interesting |
| cheap | relaxing | good for your health |

Ask students to write down one noun they would associate with each adjective, e.g. *fast – car*. Then go round the class, asking individual students to say their nouns in random order, and the others must guess which adjective they go with.

1 Students should do the task individually, then compare answers before checking back with you.

> **Richard:** car is more relaxing than train; train is often late or cancelled
> **Virginia:** train is cheaper, quicker, and safer than car

2 This activity can be done in pairs, or as a class survey where students get up and ask several people the same questions. In the latter case, students can prepare a simple grid with spaces for noting the answers of all the people questioned, and results can be pooled and analysed afterwards.

B

1 Let students do the task in pairs, then pool answers with the whole class.

> plane, helicopter, coach, lorry (US = truck), bicycle, motorbike, moped, boat, ferry

2 Let students do this individually, then compare answers before checking back with you.

| slow | expensive | unhealthy | stressful / tiring |
| boring | difficult | bad for ... | |

3 Do this as a whole-class activity. Answers are quite subjective in some cases, so there may be some disagreement.

C

1 Do this as a whole-class activity. Answers are subjective, so accept any sentence as long as it is justified with an appropriate reason.

2 Elicit the rule from the class, then refer them to the Language Note. To test their understanding, ask them what the comparative form would be for the other adjectives they saw in **B**. Point out that we only use *less* with adjectives of two or more syllables. We cannot say *A is less big than B*; instead we say *A isn't as big as B*.

> *-er* is used for adjectives of one syllable (NB one-syllable adjectives ending in vowel + consonant double the consonant, e.g. *big – bigger, wet – wetter*)
> *more* ... is used for adjectives of two syllables or more

3 Let students write their sentences individually. Then refer them to the example dialogue and ask them to have similar conversations with a partner.

D 51

Play the first sentence, and point out that the stressed words are underlined. Ask individual students to repeat. If they have trouble producing a complete sentence, build it up gradually, giving them a series of models which they repeat after you: *The car's ... The car's quicker ... ... quicker than the bus ... The car's quicker than the bus.* Repeat the same procedure for the other sentences.

E 52

1 Ask students to look at the photos of the three cities, and then discuss the questions as a whole class.

2 Play the tape once or twice as necessary. Students compare answers before checking back with you.

	Country	Average living area	Average rent
1	Japan	31 m^2	higher
2	USA	59 m^2	cheaper
3	France	37 m^2	more expensive / cheaper

3 Tell students to complete the sentences individually, then to look at the Language Note to check their answers. Test their understanding by going back to the list of adjectives in **B**, and asking them what the superlative form would be.

> **2** the smallest **4** the most expensive
> **3** the cheapest

4 Do this as a whole-class activity. This may involve students giving further details, particularly in a multilingual class.

Optional extra activity
Ask students to write a short report describing housing in their own country, e.g. What is the cheapest / most expensive type of housing? Is it easier to buy housing in the city or in the country? They can present their information to the class in the next lesson.

F

1 Ask students to complete the task individually, then compare answers before checking back with you. Then ask them to answer the questions in pairs.

> **2** most stressful   **6** best
> **3** earliest   **7** worst
> **4** latest   **8** most important
> **5** biggest

2 Let students do the matching exercise individually, then compare answers with a partner before checking with you. Then they should complete the questionnaire individually. Explain that they have to choose one of the four options, even if it doesn't correspond exactly to the answer they would normally give.

> **1** C **2** D **3** B **4** G **5** H **6** A **7** E **8** F

3 Ask students to compare answers with a partner. Then they should calculate their score by referring to File W on page 153. Finally, do a class survey of the results.

G 53

This gives further practice in understanding comparative and superlative forms, and develops students' speaking skills. Play the sentences one by one, repeating each one if necessary. When everybody has understood, ask individual students to give their opinion.

7.2 Describing products and services

A

Start by asking the whole class what constitutes good and bad service in a hotel and a restaurant. Then ask them to read the initial rubric. Check understanding by asking them when they last called a customer service number.

1 Ask students to read the document and then to discuss points 1–4 in pairs. Do a whole-class feedback by asking them to say which customer service promises are particularly important to them, and why.

2 Do this as a whole-class activity. If your students don't work for a company, go straight on to the next exercise.

B

1 Refer students to the NorthWest Power text. Elicit which telecommunications companies operate in their countries. Then ask them to read the text and answer the questions individually. Check answers.

> **1** a carry out b schedule c updated d allows
> **2** 12,500 (= 5 jobs per technician per day)
> **3** speed / possibility of advance planning / choosing the right person for the job

2 Explain that the diagram is in the right order, but the written description is not. Let students complete the task individually, then compare answers in pairs before checking back with you.

> The order is C, F, D, A, E, G, B.

Language Note
Give students time to read this. To check understanding, ask them to transform the two passive sentences in Part 3 into an active form, i.e. *Our team of technicians carry out ... The Work Manager arranges ...* Then ask them if the Work Manager description they have just read is in the active or passive form.

C

Ask students to complete the sentences individually, referring back to the original text where necessary.

> **1** A request for help is received by the Customer Service Department.
> **2** This request is sent to the Work Finder.
> **3** The details of the call are passed (by the Work Finder) to the Power Planner.
> **4** The work of the technicians is monitored by the Power Planner.
> **5** The work schedule is arranged (by the Power Planner), and the information is sent back to the Work Finder.
> **6** The technicians are given their schedules by the Work Finder.

38 Teacher's Book

Optional extra activity

Ask students to work in pairs and to describe the operation of a system in their own company. Those who are not yet in work could describe a simple process in everyday life, e.g. the making of a cup of tea.

D 54a

1 Ask students to read the instructions and look at the pictures. Ask them to guess why the system is called 'Veggie Vision' (note that *veg* or *veggie* is short for *vegetable*). Then they should identify the items in the pictures, which will allow you to check that they understand the words and phrases.

2 Give students time to read the questions, then play 54a once or twice as necessary. Let them compare answers before checking back with the whole class.

> 1 It identifies fruit and vegetables in the supermarket and gives the price.
> 2 cashiers at the checkout
> 3 speed
> 4 It's intelligent – it learns from its mistakes.

3 Play 54b for students to make notes and to answer the question. Check answers with the whole class.

> When Veggie Vision can't identify the item, it shows the cashier two different items, and he / she chooses the correct one.

4 Play 54b again without stopping. Then listen again, pausing after each sentence containing one of the target phrases, and ask students for the phrase. Ask them if they know any other phrases which could be used in place of those given, e.g. *Firstly, Following this, After that, Last of all, Lastly*.

> 1 First of all …   3 After this …   5 And finally …
> 2 Next …   4 Then …

5 First, ask students to work in pairs to combine elements from A and B, and to put them in order. Check with the whole class. Then ask them to write a description of the process using the passive form. Monitor, asking students to self-correct if you spot any errors.

> First of all the product is scanned by the cashier. A photo is taken of the product, and information about its size etc. is recorded. Next, the product details are compared with the database. After this, the correct item is selected (by Veggie Vision). Then the cashier is shown a picture of the item. Finally, the choice is confirmed by the cashier.

E

Let students complete the task in pairs. Then go round the class, asking each student to produce a different sentence.

Possible answers:
Microsoft software is used in 85% of the world's computers.
Bordeaux wine is produced in the south-west of France.
Rice is grown / produced in China.
Italian is spoken in parts of Switzerland.
50% of banks are robbed on a Friday.
Steak is eaten rare, medium, or well done.
The Coca-Cola company is based in Atlanta.
38 million banknotes are printed / produced in the USA every day.
The US Open tennis championships are played at Flushing Meadow.

7.3 Evaluating products

A

This exercise introduces and practises the vocabulary for describing size and dimension. Start by drawing a cube on the board.

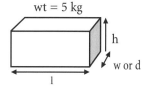

Ask students what the letters *wt*, *w* or *d*, *l* and *h* stand for. Point out that the choice of dimensions depends on the shape and which way you are looking at the object (e.g. *depth* can represent the distance from the front to the back of an object, and is also used as the opposite of *height* when describing, for example, the level of water in a swimming pool).

1 Refer students to the photo of the camera. Ask them what type of camera it is and how it is different from a traditional camera (it's digital, which means that photos can be reproduced on a computer). Then refer them to the box, and elicit what the words in each column have in common. Deal with any vocabulary comprehension problems by drawing simple pictures (columns A and C), or by showing objects in the classroom that have these qualities (columns B and D).

Then let students complete the task, comparing answers in pairs before checking back with you.

1	width; height; depth	4	rectangular
2	weight	5	grey
3	metal; glass; plastic		

2 Do the first item as a whole-class activity, then let students describe the other objects in pairs. Be ready to supply any words that are not in the list. When they have finished, choose one pair of students to give a description of each object to the whole class.

Possible answers:
desk: 80 cm in height, 80 cm to 1m 40 in length, 60 cm to 1 m in depth / width, made of metal, wood, or composite material, rectangular or square, grey or brown
golf ball: 5 cm in diameter, made of plastic, rubber, or composite material, round, white or orange
TV remote control: 10 cm in length, 4 cm in width, 1 cm in thickness, made of plastic, metal, and composite material, rectangular, black or grey
soft drink can: 5 cm in diameter, 10 cm in height, made of metal, cylindrical, silver / multi-coloured

3 Refer to the list of words you made on the board (if there are any), and ask students if they needed any more, e.g. *composite material*. Add them to your list.

4 Ask students to read Parts 1 and 2 of the Language Note. Point out that there are two ways of asking about and describing dimensions, using either the noun or adjective form. They should also notice that the words *diameter* and *weight* are different, as neither of them have an adjective form.

Focus also on the pronunciation of the different terms, where the /aɪ/ and /ɪ/ distinction often poses a problem. Ask students to group the words according to the pronunciation of the vowel sound, i.e. /e/ length, depth; /aɪ/ height, diameter, high, wide; /ɪ/ width, thick, thickness. Then ask students to complete the sentences individually with reference to the Language Note. Let them compare answers before checking back with you. Make sure they pronounce the words correctly when giving you the answers.

1	length	3	weigh	5	width	7	thick
2	high	4	depth	6	diameter		

5 Let students do the task in pairs before checking with File B on page 150. As a follow-up, you could ask each pair to think of three similar general knowledge questions which they then ask the class.

1	over 6,400 km	5	About 29 km
2	432.3 metres	6	10.3 cm
3	1.4 kg	7	Between 7 and 10 cm
4	3,926 metres		

B 55

This exercise provides practice in understanding an oral description of a product's physical qualities, and introduces *it's used for + -ing*.

Start by referring students briefly to Part 3 of the Language Note. Ask them what the example sentence *It's used for changing channels on the TV* refers to. Then elicit what sentences they could make with the same structure for the other items in **2** of **A**.

Ask students to read the rubric. Explain that there are seven clues for each product, and that after each clue they must try to guess what the object is. Play the tape, pausing after each clue. Encourage students to try and guess, but don't tell them if their answer is right or wrong. Continue listening until the final sentence, where the answer is given.

C

This is a similar guessing game to **B**, but this time the students themselves describe the products for their partners. Divide the class into A / B pairs and refer them to the relevant file. Explain that each student has half the words for the crossword and they have to give their partner clues as in the example dialogue. Ask them to transfer the words they have on to the crossword grid, without showing their partner. With a stronger class, you can start the activity immediately; with a weaker class, ask them to write out their clues beforehand so you can help with vocabulary and / or ideas.

Answers are in Files J and V on pages 151 and 153 of the Student's Book.

D 56

To introduce the topic, ask students to make a list of products or services which are designed to improve our health, e.g. vitamin pills, low-fat and sugar-free food and drink, etc. Pool ideas on the board, giving help with vocabulary where necessary.

1 Refer students to the initial rubric and the pictures of the three gifts, and ask them for their initial reaction. Let them work in pairs to discuss the possible advantages and disadvantages of each promotional gift, then feed back as a whole class.

2 Explain to students that all they have to understand is which gift the three managers choose. Play the tape once without stopping. Let them compare answers briefly before checking back with you.

> They choose the Relax-Max CD.

3 Ask the whole class if they remember any of the advantages and disadvantages mentioned. Draw the table on the board and write in any points they remember. Then play the tape once or twice more, giving them time to compare answers after each complete listening. Complete the table on the board with the whole class, then ask them if they agree with the three managers' evaluation.

> **Calorie Counter:**
> *Advantages:* cheap, lots of interesting information in it, doesn't weigh much
> *Disadvantages:* only interests women, men don't want to count calories
> **Pedometer:**
> *Advantages:* very original, useful for men and women who go running
> *Disadvantages:* expensive, doesn't give the right image
> **Relax Max CD:**
> *Advantages:* not expensive, interests men and women, not just a sports product

4 Ask students to read the Language Note, then play the tape again without stopping. Let students compare answers together, then check back with you. Play the tape again to identify which words are stressed, stopping after each target phrase. Point out that there is a tendency to stress the personal pronoun or possessive adjective: *I* think ..., What's **your** view on this?, If you ask **me** ...

> Expressions used (stressed words in bold): I think ... What do **you** think? ... I don't agree ... I think you're right ... In **my** view ... I disagree ... I don't think ... I agree ... I think so too

E

In this exercise students have to simulate a meeting to decide on various marketing issues relating to a new chocolate bar. They will have the opportunity to practise the language for expressing opinions, the vocabulary of size and dimension, and comparative forms. Refer students to the rubric. Point out that they are responsible for marketing a low-calorie chocolate bar, so it is supposed to be sold as a 'healthy' product. Explain that the first thing they will have to do is decide on their target market, and all the other decisions will depend on that. Refer them to the agenda, and deal with any problems of vocabulary.

Give students 15 minutes to prepare some thoughts individually on the different points, then divide the class into groups of three (you may prefer to have slightly larger meeting groups). Set a time limit of 30 minutes for the meeting, and tell them they must cover every point on the agenda. Explain that you will ask for a summary of their meeting at the end, so they must make notes.

Monitor, noting any mistakes you hear, particularly in the use of the target language for this unit. Deal with these at the end of the lesson, or in a later lesson if you feel some remedial work is necessary.

At the end of the meeting, ask each group to give a summary of their decisions, with reasons. Encourage the other groups to react to the views of the presenting group.

Photocopiable activity (page 73)
This gives further practice in describing the physical qualities and functions of different objects. Divide the class into groups of four, and give each person in the group a different invention to describe. Check that they understand the vocabulary in the instructions. Explain that they have to persuade their colleagues to invest money in it. Give them ten to fifteen minutes to prepare a presentation. Start by writing up the following questions as a guide to what should go into their description:

What is your invention used for?
What's it made of?
What size is it? Are there different sizes or models?
Does it come in different colours?
How does it work?
Who are the customers?
Where do you want to sell it?
How much does it cost?

Students then describe their inventions to each other. Encourage those listening to ask further questions or to raise objections. At the end each group should vote on the best invention.

Unit 8 | Life stories

8.1 Success stories

A

The two people featured in this section both have connections with air travel. Juan Trippe was the founder of Pan Am and Barbara Cassani was the first CEO of Go. The first exercise is a vocabulary warmer on the theme of air travel. You can precede this by brainstorming words to do with air travel, and writing them on the board.

1. Let students do the activity in pairs before checking back with you.

> 1 airports
> 2 airlines
> 3 aircraft / aeroplanes (US = airplanes)
> 4 destinations
> 5 passengers
> 6 return (US = round trip)
> 7 flight
> 8 book
> 9 class
> 10 take off

2. If you didn't start with the brainstorming session then do this now.

B

1. See if students know anything about Trippe before they read the text. Then give them three minutes to read and answer the question. Ask them not to stop at words they do not understand.

> His company introduced the first transatlantic flights and was one of the first to offer cheap air travel around the world. Trippe helped develop the jet engine for commercial flights and influenced the development of the Jumbo Jet.

2. Check understanding of the vocabulary in the questions. Encourage student–student explanations and use of monolingual dictionaries. Remind students of the glossary at the back of the book. Let them work in pairs to answer the questions. Check answers with the whole class.

> 1 Yale
> 2 Wall Street
> 3 1927
> 4 at the end of the thirties
> 5 They wanted to keep prices high and earn maximum profit.
> 6 Longer distances could be covered more quickly.
> 7 It could carry more passengers per flight.
> 8 He ordered too many 747s and put Pan Am into financial difficulties.

3. This activity focuses on time expressions. Write two pairs of expressions on the board which have the same meaning.

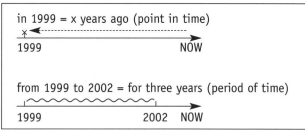

If students have problems understanding *ago* and *for*, draw time lines as in the board plan above. Let students work in pairs to complete the task. Feed back as a whole class. Refer them to the Language Note for further clarification.

> 1 thirteen years later   6 the following year
> 2 from 1924 to 1926   7 For several years
> 3 after the Second World War 8 in 1899
> 4 in 1958   9 eight years later
> 5 In the sixties

C [57]

1. Ask students if they know the names of any other cheap airlines such as Easy-jet, Buzz, Ryan Air, etc. Elicit why they are popular and why they are different to other airlines. Read the rubric and play the tape once for students to order the events.

> a 3   b 6   c 1   d 7   e 4   f 5   g 2

Play the tape again and look at some of the language used. Concentrate on the simple past active forms used, e.g. *Robert Ayling **decided** to create a low-cost airline.*

2 Let students do the task individually and then check back with you.

1 e	3 c	5 d	7 b
2 f	4 a	6 g	

D 58a

1 This exercise introduces the past passive form. Read the initial rubric then play 58a for students to complete the notes. Feed back with the whole class.

Birth: US, 1960
Education: first degree Massachusetts, Masters at Princeton
Husband: British
First vacation job: worked for a US Senator in 1981
First post abroad: 1986
1987: joined BA
1992: had her first baby
1993: General Manager of BA in New York
1997: CEO of Go

Listen to the tape again and ask students to repeat the key phrases.

2 Play 58b for students to listen for the missing phrases. They are all in the passive form. Elicit why the passive is used. Refer them to the Language Note for clarification.

1 She was transferred	3 She was appointed
2 She was offered	

Language Note
Stress that the passive is usually used when we do not know, or do not care, who did a particular action. If we do want to say who did it but continue to stress the action itself we use *by*, e.g. *St Paul's was designed by Sir Christopher Wren.*

E

This exercise requires an authentic mix of passive and active sentences. Students should use the dates and words in the box to write a short history of Barbara Cassani.

Optional extra activity
Ask students to write a short history about themselves or someone they know. They could do this as a homework task and report back in the next lesson.

F

1 This activity can be done with the whole class. Write the table on the board and ask students to make six questions, using each verb once.

2 Let students work in pairs to ask and answer the *When ...?* questions they have made in **1**. They should also ask a *Where ...?* question as in the example dialogue. Check answers (see the answers for **3**).

3 Using the information in the box, they can now make *Who ... by?* questions and ask and answer them in pairs.

The telephone was invented by Alexander Graham Bell in the US in 1875.
The Channel Tunnel was built by Eurotunnel 40 metres under the seabed in 1994.
The Titanic was launched in Belfast by Cammells Shipyard in 1912.
Sony was founded by Akio Morita in Tokyo in 1946.
Penicillin was discovered by Alexander Fleming in London in 1928.
The Beatles were formed in Liverpool by John Lennon and Paul McCartney in 1962.

As a homework task, ask students to write five more questions about famous discoveries or inventions.

8.2 Making money

This section focuses on financial language. It has been designed for non-specialists to teach, and to be of interest to those students who do not necessarily use such language in their professional lives. Try to use your students' knowledge to get the most out of the section.

A

To introduce the topic, look at the cartoon and brainstorm as many words connected with money as you can.

 Ask students to read the rubric. Demonstrate the task by writing sentences on the board, with an invented word in a key position. Elicit the meaning of the invented words.

It was a beautiful sunny day and there was not a single *splog* in the sky.
Dollars, euros, and yen are all *goppules*.

Ask students to cover the words in the box and then read the text and see how many of the missing words they can guess. Feed back as a whole class and then ask them to complete the text, using the words in the box. Check answers.

Teacher's Book   43

1 invested	8 earn
2 shares	9 tax
3 dividend	10 lent
4 stake	11 owe
5 shareholders	12 pay
6 worth	13 spend
7 borrowed	14 save

As a homework task, ask students to make more sentences using the words in the box. Encourage them to make up sentences which illustrate the meaning of the words. This will help students to remember them more easily.

2 This activity checks understanding of the vocabulary in **1**. It can be done as a whole-class activity.

1 F   2 F   3 T   4 F   5 F   6 T   7 F   8 T

B

This exercise combines language work and logic plus a little arithmetic.

1 Establish that there are five shareholders in the company: A, B, C, D and E, and that the total number of shares remains at 1,000 throughout. Let students work in pairs to work out the number of shares and complete the pie chart. Make sure they read and count carefully! Feed back as a class, putting the information from the sentences on the board.

1994	1,000 shares in the company. All owned by A **A = 1,000 shares**
1995	A sold 20% (200 shares) to B and C, $^3/_4$ to B and $^1/_4$ to C **A = 800, B = 150, C = 50**
1996	D bought 25% of A's shares **A = 600, B = 150, C = 50, D = 200**
1998	E bought half of B's shares (75) **A = 600, B = 75, C = 50, D = 200, E = 75**

A owns 60%	(600 shares)
D owns 20%	(200 shares)
B and E own 7.5%	(75 shares each)
C owns 5%	(50 shares)

2 Let students complete the task in pairs then check their answers in File A on page 150.

1 A got 600 × £20 = £12,000
   B got 75 × £20 = £1,500
   C got 50 × £20 = £1,000
   D got 200 × £20 = £4,000
   E got 75 × £20 = £1,500

2 He bought the shares for £10,000 in 1996. He got a dividend of £4,000 in 1999. The company is now valued at £200,000 so his stake is worth £40,000. Quite a good investment!
3 A is the majority shareholder (60%).
4 E's share is worth 7.5% of £200,000 = £15,000.

C   [59]

This exercise checks comprehension of dates and amounts. Students should write the numbers as figures rather than words.

1 Play the tape once for students to write down the dates.

2 Play the tape again for them to write down the amounts.

3 Play a third time for students to complete the sentences.

1 1977; $78,300,000
2 1899; 5 cents
3 1867; $7,000,000
4 $100,000,000; 1877
5 1995; £2,474,655,000
6 1986; $3,080,000

D

This exercise continues the topic of money and practises some of the vocabulary from the section.

1 Ask students to read the text individually and try to answer the questions. Check answers and deal with any vocabulary problems.

1 b   2 b   3 a   4 c   5 a

2 Point out that the numbers listed are not always in the same form as in the text. Let students do the task individually then compare in pairs before checking back with you.

a Prince Alwaleed's percentage shareholdings in Citicorp and Apple
b his age when he ran his first company
c his percentage stake in Disneyland
d the year he bought his shares in Citicorp
e the price he paid in dollars for the Citicorp shares
f what he was worth in dollars by 1988
g what his stake in Citicorp is now worth
h the amount of his investment in the Kingdom Centre

As a follow-up activity, ask students to summarize the article orally.

E [60]

1 Ask students to look at the headlines and check comprehension. Explain that they are going to listen to some news stories and have to match them to the headlines. Play the tape for students to do the matching, then check answers with the whole class.

1 b	2 d	3 a	4 c

2 Ask students to look at the comprehension questions and see how many they can answer. There are two for each story. Play the tape again and collate answers as a class.

1 £70 million	5 0.25%
2 £3.50	6 shares fell
3 Swedish	7 Allianz is buying AGF
4 for their annual bonus	8 Germany

F

This exercise allows less controlled practice of financial vocabulary. Students should work in pairs to complete the sentences in the most interesting or amusing way possible. Encourage some fun.

G

Let students work in pairs to find the collocations, then feed back with the whole class.

money: spend, save, earn, borrow, lend, give, owe, invest, lose, inherit
pay: rent, salaries, back, for, tax, a dividend

8.3 Company history

A

1 Ask students to look at the logos and see how many they recognize. Go through each of the questions, establishing which brands / companies / logos are famous in particular countries.

2 As a further example of a strong brand, this activity focuses on McDonald's. Let students work in pairs to do the quiz, then collate answers with the whole class.

B [61a]

1 Play the tape once. It is a long listening so tell students not to worry if they do not understand everything. Check answers.

1 1955	6 1965
2 1968	7 5 hours
3 1999	8 40,000,000
4 1963	9 1979
5 90 seconds	10 100

2 Play the tape again to complete the gaps in the sentences. Let them compare in pairs before checking back with you. Play the tape again in chunks, and ask them to focus on the verbs, noting which are in the passive.

1955	opened; bought
1963	appeared
1965	was floated; cost
1967	opened
1968	was launched
1979	was introduced
1990	opened
1995	was acquired; increased
1999	was opened

3 Refer students to the Language Note, checking they can form passive questions correctly. Let them work in pairs to do the task. Remind them that in company histories and annual reports the passive is often used. Let them compare in pairs before checking back with you.

1. When did Ray Croc open his first restaurant?
2. When did Ronald McDonald appear on TV?
3. When was the company floated?
4. How much did 100 shares cost?
5. When was the Big Mac launched?
6. When was the Happy Meal introduced?
7. When did Ray Croc die?
8. Where did McDonald's restaurants open in 1990?
9. When was Burghy acquired?
10. Where was the 25,000th restaurant opened?

C

Divide the class into A / B pairs and refer them to the relevant files. Each student has information on the history of a different company (Student A: Estée Lauder; Student B: Sony). Elicit the questions required to find out the information, e.g.:

– *When was the company founded?*
– *Who was it founded by?*
– *Where is it based?*
– *What is the activity of the company?*
– *Does it have any famous products?*
– *Do you know any important dates in its history?*

Monitor, noting examples of good language and any mistakes. Feed back with the whole class.

D

This activity can be given as a homework task or done in class. It focuses on word families for some of the vocabulary covered in the section. It is also useful preparation for the presentation to be made in **E**.

> **Verb:** found; acquire; introduce; expand
> **Noun:** increase; launch; creation; opening
> **Example:** founded; acquired; increased; launch; created; introduced; openings; expansion

E

1 Read through the information about Henry Ford and check comprehension. Let students work in pairs to prepare a presentation. Monitor, making sure they use a mix of active and passive verb forms.

2 This activity allows students to make their own presentations about the history of a company they know. Those who do not have knowledge of a company should use the histories in the files in **C**. Ask for volunteers to present their companies.

3 Ask students to look at the photos and try to match them to the names. Then let them work in pairs to match the years and the other information to the relevant names. They can find the answers in File L on page 152.

Photocopiable activity (page 74)

Cut up the words on page 74 and use them for the following categorizing activities.

1 Find four pairs of opposites.
2 Find five words which go with *bank*.
3 Find five words which go with *rate*.
4 Find all the words with one syllable.
5 Find all the verbs.

Then use the same words for defining games. Ask the students to work in pairs and divide the words into two piles. Students have one minute to define as many of the words as possible without revealing the spelling.

> **1** borrow, lend
> spend, save
> credit, debit
> buy / purchase, sell
> profit, loss
> income, expenditure
>
> **2** bank card
> bank account
> bank loan
> bank payment
> bank book
>
> **3** interest rate
> exchange rate
> inflation rate
> tax rate
> bank rate
> credit rate
>
> **4** shares owe   lose   spend earn   tax
> rate   save stocks lend   card   credit
> pay   rent cheque bank   loan   loss
> rise   buy   sell   sales book   date
>
> **5** owe lose spend earn save lend
> pay rent bank   rise buy   sell
> book

Unit 9 | Dealing with problems

9.1 Making decisions

A `62a`

This exercise serves to highlight the difference between the present continuous for future use and *will* for spontaneous decisions. Introduce the theme by asking students to list reasons why people travel for business, e.g. to visit a supplier, to prospect for new business, etc.

1 Refer students to the rubric, then ask them to complete the task individually. Let them compare answers in pairs before checking back with you.

> 1 in Germany
> 2 Katya Muster (Assistant to the President)
> 3 arrange a schedule of visits for Frau Köhnen

2 Play `62a` once or twice as necessary, allowing students to compare answers before checking back with you.

> 1 4th   5 clients
> 2 11th   6 Wednesday
> 3 sales conference   7 Thursday
> 4 staff   8 1

3 First see if students can remember / suggest possible words to complete the gaps. Then play `62a` again, stopping after each target sentence for students to fill the gaps. Check answers with the whole class. Ask them which tense is used (present continuous) and why (the speakers are talking about future arrangements).

> is coming; is ... staying; Is ... spending; she's arriving

4 Ask students to read the rubric, then play `62b` once or twice as necessary. Let them compare notes before checking back with you.

> reserve a hotel room; travel arrangements; meet her at station or airport; is she leaving on Thursday; reserve a room; prepare a provisional schedule

5 Ask students if they can remember which verb form is used in the two example sentences, then listen to the first part of `62b` to check. Play the rest of the tape, pausing after all other examples of *I'll* and *We'll* to allow students to tell you what was said. Ask them to read the Language Note to find out why the speakers use the *will* form (because the speakers are making a decision at the time of speaking).

> I'll phone, I'll see. Other examples: I'll ask ..., I'll check ..., I'll reserve ..., We'll talk ...

Optional extra activity
Divide the class into A / B pairs and tell them to imagine that they work together in a company. Student A should think of a person who is making a visit to the company and should list date / time of arrival, etc. and any other relevant information. Student B should then ask questions to elicit the information. Finally both students should plan who is going to do what for the visit. Monitor, checking that students are using both the present continuous and *will*.

B

Refer students to the rubric and the first example, then ask the whole class for an alternative answer to number 1. Then let them complete the task in pairs. Ask them to try and find two solutions for each problem. Monitor, making sure they are using the contracted *I'll* form, and not *I will*. When they have finished, do a whole-class feedback on possible answers.

> **Possible answers:**
> 2 I'll fly Economy class.
> 3 I'll buy a present.
> 4 I'll fly with a different airline.
> 5 I'll hire a car.
> 6 I'll meet his colleague.
> 7 I'll stay in bed!

C `63`

1 Ask students to predict what words could be missing in the sentences. This will help them to revise tense forms as well as giving practice in saying different contractions. Then play the tape once without stopping. Give students time to compare answers before playing again, sentence by sentence, and asking them for the correct answer.

> 1 I'll   3 They aren't   5 You're   7 When's he
> 2 She's   4 We'll   6 He's not

2 Let students do this in pairs, listening to each other's pronunciation and correcting each other as necessary.

D

This exercise introduces and practises verbs associated with administrative organization. Before you start, ask students to imagine that they are responsible for planning a conference. What kind of things will they need to do in preparation for it?

1 Ask students to complete the checklist with the words in the box. Let them compare answers with a partner before checking back with you. Ask them if there are any other things that should be in the list, e.g. confirm the number of hotel rooms, invite the press.

1 book	4 remind	7 send	10 make
2 invite	5 hire	8 order	11 pick up
3 ask	6 print	9 check	12 take

2 Let students complete this in pairs, then collate answers on the board.

> **Possible answers:**
> **to check:** an invoice / a bill / that everything is OK
> **to order:** a drink in a bar / some office supplies / a meal in a restaurant
> **to hire:** a car / audio-visual equipment / a security guard
> **to send:** a fax / an e-mail / a letter
> **to invite:** someone for dinner / to your home / for the weekend

E 64

1 Ask students to read the dialogue and predict what words could fill the gaps. Then play the tape once through without stopping. Let them compare answers, then play again, sentence by sentence. Note that most of the missing words are unstressed, so you may need to guide students towards the answer, pointing out that *can* is pronounced /kən/ and *shall* as /ʃəl/. Ask follow-up questions to check their understanding, e.g. *Why is A booking the hotel rooms?*

> Can, shall; Can; Shall, I'll; can

2 Answer this question quickly with the whole class, then refer them to the Language Note. Elicit a few more examples of *Shall I ...?* by giving some cues and asking students to offer you help, e.g. *I'm thirsty.*

Play the tape once again and ask students to identify which words are particularly stressed (principally the personal pronouns *you* and *I*). Ask them to repeat the conversation twice, swapping roles the second time.

3 Read the rubric and the Person A / B information with students, and deal with any vocabulary problems. Then ask students to go through the checklist of points in **C**, and decide whether A or B is the best person to do each task (or put *?* if it doesn't matter who). Let students compare answers in pairs before checking back with you. Then ask them to repeat the original conversation in **1** and continue from there. Monitor, asking students to self-correct mistakes in grammatical form or sentence stress.

9.2 Thinking ahead

A

As a warmer, bring in some magazine adverts for different products. Ask students to identify what type of customer the product or service is aimed at, where it is sold, and how it is advertised (apart from in magazines). You can use this as a way of teaching some of the target vocabulary.

1 Let students complete this individually, then compare answers in pairs before checking back with you.

> **Customers:** retired people, business people, the general public, companies, the 20–30 age group
> **Distribution:** department stores, shopping centres, supermarkets, specialist shops, mail order
> **Advertising:** newspapers, specialist magazines, hoardings, TV and radio adverts, direct mailing

2 Do this as a whole-class activity, writing suggestions on the board.

> **Possible answers:**
> **Customers:** 40–50, etc. age group, teenagers, children, single men / women, married couples
> **Distribution:** wholesalers, boutiques, factory outlets
> **Advertising:** women's magazines, sports magazines, word of mouth

3 Let students do this in pairs then feed back as a class.

B 65

1 Refer students to the picture and the accompanying product description. Check vocabulary comprehension, then teach the word *features* by contrasting with the word *benefits*. Ask for examples of features and corresponding benefits for a car, e.g. turbo engine – improves acceleration. Students should then complete the task and answer the follow-up questions in pairs. Check answers with the whole class.

48   Teacher's Book

1 stopwatch	3 voice record, playback
2 world time: 24 time zones	4 calculator

Other features and benefits:
- 50 pages of telememo: you can write messages for yourself to remind you to do things
- 5 multi-function alarms: you can use them to wake yourself up or to remind you that it's time to finish a meeting
- auto-calendar: you can check the dates of public holidays for the next few years

2 Start by asking students what customers, outlets, and advertising media they would choose for the DBCV501. Then play the tape once or twice as necessary, giving them time to compare answers before checking with you.

Types of customer: business people who travel, particularly men in the 20–35 age group
Sales outlets: airport shopping centres, mail order
Advertising: specialist press (business magazines), direct mailing

3 Play the tape again, stopping after each target sentence to give students time to write. Elicit the answers, playing individual sentences again if necessary. Check understanding of *won't* (students may have written *want*).

you'll, won't; Will; won't; we'll

4 Give students a minute to match the sentences, then play the tape again to check. Answer the follow-up questions as a whole-class activity. Ask students why the speakers in the dialogue don't use the present continuous (because they're not talking about future arrangements). Explain that here they use *will* because they are making predictions. Refer them to the Language Note on page 108.

1 c 2 a 3 b
- the present simple
- the future with *will* or *won't*
- when the sentence begins with *if*

C

1 Elicit a few ideas for this from the whole class.

2 Do the first two sentences with the whole class, then let them complete the task in pairs, first orally, then in writing.

If we have more contact with customers, we'll sell more banking services.
If we sell more banking services, we'll increase our turnover.
If we close less profitable branches, it won't be necessary to recruit more staff.
If it isn't necessary to recruit more staff, our salary costs won't rise.
If we need staff all day Saturday, the unions probably won't accept / will probably reject it.
If the unions don't accept / reject it, we'll offer the staff longer holidays.

Optional extra activity
Write the following sentences on the board.

If the weather's bad this weekend, …
I'll call you if …
If I have enough time, …
They won't sign the contract if …
If we leave now, …
You'll earn a lot of money if …

Ask students to think of phrases to complete each sentence. They should then say their phrases in random order to a partner, who must guess which sentence he / she is completing.

D 66

1 Let students write the contracted forms, then compare notes with a partner, saying them aloud. Check answers with the whole class quickly.

A	B
1 I'm not	1 I haven't
2 She's not / She isn't	2 She's got
4 Who'll work	3 I won't sell
5 We'll buy	4 Who's working
8 They're not / They aren't	6 I'd like
	8 There aren't

2 Play the tape once without stopping, then give students time to compare answers. Then play again sentence by sentence and ask students for the answers. With a stronger class, ask them to reproduce the whole sentence.

1 B 2 A 3 B 4 A 5 B 6 B 7 A 8 A

E

This exercise practises reading for specific information. Ask students to read the eight predictions, and deal with any vocabulary problems. Ask them how accurate they think each prediction is. Then ask them to do the matching task. Check answers with the whole class, asking what words or phrases helped them reach their conclusions. Ask if they agree with the experts' conclusions.

a 8   b 3   c 6   d 1   e 2   f 7   g 4   h 5

9.3 Complaining and apologizing

A

This exercise introduces vocabulary used for complaining and apologizing in a professional situation. Start by brainstorming reasons for calling a supplier to complain.

1 Ask students to match the people to the situations. Let them compare answers in pairs before checking with you. Check comprehension of target vocabulary: *break down* (for a machine), *an order / to order, to place an order, to overcharge* (opposite = *undercharge*), *a record of ...* (= written reference of a payment, an order, etc.).

1 C   2 B   3 D   4 F   5 H   6 A   7 E   8 G

2 Refer students to the example sentence and ask why they need to use *I'll*. Then let them do this individually and compare answers in pairs. Check difficult vocabulary: *transporter, dispatch, credit note*. Check answers with the whole class, asking which phrases are used to apologize. Point out that in English-speaking cultures, people tend to use the phrases *I'm afraid ...* and *I'm sorry ...* much more than other nationalities use the equivalent expressions.

The answers match the responses (a–h) to the complaints (A–H) and the situations (1–8).
a B2   c H5   e F4   g C1   b D3   d G8   f A6   h E7

B [67]

1 Refer students to the memo and ask what information is needed to complete it. Then play [67a] once or twice as necessary, giving them time to compare answers before checking back with you.

Caller: Steve Meehan   **Company:** TPS   **Order N°:** 4189/JG   **Description:** 20 calculators model RK 529   **Problem:** no instruction manuals   **Action:** call back in 10–15 minutes

2 Play [67b] once or twice as necessary, giving students time to compare answers before checking back with you.

The instruction manuals are still in the factory; she will send them by express mail today.

3 Let students do the task in pairs, then check answers with the whole class. Play [67a] and [67b] again to check. Elicit in which sentences Stephanie is saying sorry (*I do apologize ..., I'm sorry about ...*), and in which one she is giving bad news (*I'm afraid ...*). As a follow-up, ask students to reproduce the two conversations between Stephanie and the customer, using the completed complaint form as a reference. With a weaker class, ask them to turn to the tapescript on page 169 and to read that aloud in pairs first.

1 calling – C   5 sorry, but – S   2 about – S   6 Shall I – S   3 look into – C   7 apologize – S   4 I'll ... back – S

Language Note

Point out that *I'm sorry, but ...* is used to give bad news, but *I'm sorry ... (I'm late)* is used to apologize. To illustrate this, point out the difference between *I'm sorry, but I can't come tonight* and *I'm sorry I couldn't come last night*. Elicit a few more examples of *Would you like me to ...?* by giving a few more cues and asking them to offer you help, e.g. *I have a headache*.

C

This exercise practises language for making or responding to complaints on the phone. Tell students they are going to have two conversations similar to the ones they heard in **B**. Divide the class into A / B pairs and refer them to the relevant information. Ask them to read the first situation. Check comprehension by asking who is making / receiving the call, then let them role-play the conversation. Ask one pair to act out their conversation in front of the class, and use it as a basis for correction. Then follow the same procedure for the second situation.

D

This exercise highlights the formal / informal distinction in written correspondence and telephone language, still in the context of complaints, apologies, and customer service.

1 Give students two minutes to read this, then discuss answers with the whole class.

> Diana ordered 350 champagne glasses for a conference starting the next day, and a lot of them have arrived broken. Diana wants Ms Geraldo to send some replacement glasses today.

2 Focus on the formal / informal distinction by asking students why it would be inappropriate to say *Please give this matter your immediate attention* on the phone. Then let them complete the task individually, before you check answers with the whole class.

Telephone	E-mail
They arrived …	We took delivery …
Can you send …?	I would be grateful if you could send …
Can you look into …?	Please give this matter your immediate attention.
Speak to you soon.	I look forward to hearing from you.

3 Let students do the task individually, then compare answers before checking back with you. As a follow-up, ask students to role-play Diana Shining's complaint to Ms Geraldo in the form of a telephone conversation.

1 Sorry about the delay.
2 See you on 23 January.
3 I'm sorry, but / I'm afraid your order will be three days late.
4 Shall I send you some more information?
5 Have a pleasant trip.

4 Let students write the e-mail in pairs, or set it as an individual homework task. Refer them to the Language File on page 158 for further useful letter-writing expressions.

Model answer:
Dear Ms Shining,
I tried to phone you but there was no reply. I would like to apologize for the broken glasses. I am sending you some replacement glasses immediately. I would be grateful if you could phone me when they arrive.
I look forward to hearing from you.
Yours sincerely,

Optional extra activity
Ask students to imagine they are the customer in **B**, and to write a letter of complaint to Stephanie Rowe.

This exercise consolidates the language of the unit. The game is based on *noughts and crosses*. Illustrate the concept of the game by drawing a blank grid on the board, and inviting a student to play a game of *noughts and crosses* with you. Explain that students are going to play the same game, but they have to make a correct sentence to win a square. Refer them to the rubric and give them time to read the rules. Make sure they understand the difference between squares and squares, and where to find the corresponding questions. Explain that if there is disagreement over what is the correct answer, you will be the judge. Tell students to write their initials in pencil, so they can play more than one game. Note that if a student gives an incorrect sentence, his opponent can only win the square if he can give a correct version for the same question cue. If both students are wrong, don't give them the answer – let them try again when one of them next wants to win that square.

Possible answers:

⊘
1 Can I leave a message?
2 Would you like me to confirm the reservation by fax?
3 Can I take a message?
4 Students' own answers.
5 Can you hold the line please?
6 I'll put it in the post today.
7 Can you fax me this month's sales figures please?
8 Would you like me to come to your office?

⋈
A Can you meet Mr Andros at the airport?
B I'll carry your suitcase.
C Could you make 200 copies please?
D I'm … this weekend. What are you doing?
E Shall I open the window?
F Students' own answers using *I'll have …*
G Students' own answers using *I'm …*
H Excuse me, I'm going to wash my hands.

Photocopiable activity (page 75)
This gives further practice in complaints and apologies. Distribute A roles to one side of class and B roles to the other. Ask them to look at the complaint sentences on the left and discuss with a partner who is speaking, in what situation, and what a possible response might be. Then divide the class into A / B pairs. Students then take it in turns to read their complaint sentences aloud, and their partner chooses the correct response from the speech bubbles on the right.

Check answers with the whole class, including details of who is speaking and where. Finally, ask students to continue each dialogue.

Unit 10 | People at work

10.1 Suggesting and recommending

A

This exercise acts as a vocabulary pre-teaching activity. Students will need most of the vocabulary to complete the section. Ask them to work in pairs and brainstorm the words to complete the word square. It would be useful to have access to dictionaries, either monolingual or bilingual depending on the level and make-up of the class. Collate answers on the board and ask students to make example sentences to show they can use the words actively. Expand the list to include helpful collocations or words in the same family, e.g. *mailing, mailshot, mailing list, discounted price, removal, rented*, etc.

1	mail	6	staff
2	discount	7	premises
3	move	8	lease
4	rent	9	competitors
5	turnover	10	advertise

B

This exercise looks at the language of suggestions. A distinction is drawn between strong suggestions and other suggestions. Students will also learn how to respond to them.

1 Ask the class to look at the two problem letters addressed to Dr Biz. There are three 'gist' questions to answer. Ask students to read the letters quickly without worrying about vocabulary problems. Let them compare answers in pairs before checking back with you.

1	A – restaurant; B – translation agency
2	to renew his lease or not
3	to get more business

Ask students to look again at the first letter and to answer more detailed comprehension questions:

- *Where is the restaurant?*
- *Who are the customers?*
- *When is the restaurant busy / quiet?*
- *Why are the prices low?*
- *What about the building? Is it all used?*
- *Does he own the building?*
- *When does the lease finish?*

2 Read through the rubric and check students understand the situation. Ask them to work individually before checking back with the whole class. Highlight the use of the gerund after *How about* ...

> **Strong recommendations:** I would advise you to ...;
> I don't think you should ...
> **Suggestions:** How about ...?; Why don't you ...?;
> Perhaps you should ...

Optional extra activity
Write on cards a number of problems and distribute them around the class, e.g.:

- *I've lost my passport.*
- *I need to improve my English more quickly.*
- *I don't like my boss.*
- *My boss doesn't like me.*
- *I don't earn enough money.*

Ask different students to read out their problem and elicit advice from the class, using the language from Dr Biz's letter.

3 Ask students to read Astrid's letter again and check comprehension:

- *Who works with Astrid?*
- *Where is the agency based?*
- *What is the main problem?*
- *What is her marketing strategy?*
- *Can they spend more money?*

Then ask students to work in pairs to compose a reply to Astrid. Ask different pairs to read out their advice, and write some of the best ideas on the board. Compare strong suggestions with more neutral ones.

C 68

In the listening passage, Dr Biz replies to Astrid on his radio programme. Students will see if their suggestions are similar in form and content to those of the expert.

1 Play the tape and ask students to complete the gaps in the left-hand column. Check answers with the whole class.

1 I think you should
2 How about
3 Why don't you
4 I'd advise you to
5 What about

2 Play the tape again for students to complete the responses. They should also note Astrid's reasons for each response she gives. You may need to play the tape again for this. Check answers with the whole class.

1 *don't think; answer* – I don't think they have the time, or they forget.
2 *not sure* – some translator friends of ours have an Internet website, and they say the response isn't so good.
3 *No, that's; question* – we work from home, and we live about eighty kilometres from Essen. Most of our customers are in Essen, and it's just too far.
4 *Yes; possibility* – (but) we can't afford to employ any more people.
5 *Yes; good idea* – I think I'll try that.

3 Let students do the task in pairs before checking with the whole class.

1 4   2 3   3 5   4 2   5 1

Language Note
Ask students to read this to consolidate what they have just studied. They will have a further opportunity to practise the language in **D** and **E**.

D

1 This activity allows students to brainstorm solutions to problems. One solution has been suggested for each problem. Ask students to work in pairs and then do a whole-class feedback. Collate ideas on the board so all pairs have access to the best and funniest suggestions.

Possible answers:
Promote him. Let him go. Offer him a new car.
Use a new advertising agency. Advertise differently.
Introduce a smoking area. Introduce smoking times, e.g. before 8 a.m.
Offer a different incentive. Increase your prices by 5%, then give the discount.
Give his details to a head-hunter. Tell him it is time to spend time with his family.

2 Ask students to form new pairs to discuss the problems in **1**, using the cues provided for A and B.

Monitor, encouraging accurate and appropriate use of the language from the Language Note.

E

This exercise is a fun way to end the section. Divide the class into A / B pairs and refer them to the relevant file. Student A's problems are quite serious, his firm is in trouble and his staff are not happy. He is under a lot of stress. Student B on the other hand has problems of a different nature. He is rich, works for his father, and has decisions of a less stressful type to make. Let students do the activity, which might lead to a discussion on whether working for your father is a good or a bad thing.

10.2 Responsibilities and regulations

A

1 This listening activity acts as a warmer to the section. Both jobs are in fact done by the same person, as you will discover in the reading text. Play the tape sentence by sentence and ask the class to guess the jobs.

Job 1: banker
Job 2: rugby referee

2 Refer students to the rubric and ask them to read the article and answer the four comprehension questions.

1 to deal with customers telephoning them or using the Internet
2 flexible working hours
3 He can do two different jobs and travel more.
4 He can work four days a week and then be at home for three days, to look after his children so his wife can work.

Discuss with the whole class whether there are similar working conditions in their company or in firms they know.

B

1 The class already know about Roger Penn. In this activity students are listening for the form of what he says as much as the content. Play the tape, then let students compare answers in pairs before checking back with you.

Teacher's Book   53

> 1 I have to do twenty hours per week for the bank.
> 2 I can referee or train most afternoons.
> 3 I don't have to work after lunch.
> 4 You can't be too friendly.

Check understanding of the expressions by asking students to use them to make sentences about their language learning, e.g.:
– *I have to do three hours homework per week.*
– *I don't have to come to school at the weekend.*
– *I can use the language laboratory every day.*

2 See if students can answer this without listening again. If not, play the last section of the tape.

> Players have to do what he says but customers can decide for themselves.

C

1 Let students work in pairs to do this task. Monitor, encouraging them to use the new language. Feed back as a class.

> 3 You can ...
> 4 You can ...
> 5 You don't have to ...
> 6 You can ...
> 7 You can ...
> 8 You don't have to ...
> 9 You don't have to ...

2 Elicit any disadvantages from the whole class, e.g.:
– *You can't always get a pension.*
– *You have to work on a temporary contract.* etc.

Language Note
Read through this carefully with students, checking they understand and can use all the structures.

D

1 This activity gives students a chance to use modals to describe their own work situation. Ask them to work in pairs to discuss their work regulations. Refer them to the words in the box, pointing out the usefulness of *I'm not allowed to*. When they have finished, ask them to report back to the class.

2 Ask students to do the matching task individually, then to compare answers in pairs before checking back with you. Then let them work in pairs to discuss the pros and cons of each job. Feed back as a class.

> 1 b
> 2 c – has to stand up a lot; can get big tips
> 3 d – has to be patient, dynamic, successful; can meet lots of different people
> 4 e – has to work to strict deadlines; can be very creative
> 5 a – has to be nice to everybody; can read during quiet times
> 6 f – has to work antisocial hours; can earn a lot of money

3 Everybody has both advantages and disadvantages in their job. Ask students to discuss their jobs in pairs and report back to the rest of the class.

E 71

1 This activity allows the class to learn some of the key vocabulary in the reading text. They can look at the text to see the words in context if they need any help. Let students compare in pairs before checking back with you.

> 1 h   4 i   7 c
> 2 e   5 a   8 b
> 3 f   6 d   9 g

2 Refer students to the rubric and check comprehension. Ask them to read the text quickly. Then ask one or two comprehension questions:
– *Is it a strict company?*
– *Does it treat employees kindly?*
– *Who is the most important, staff or customers?*

Let students complete the activity in pairs and then report back to the whole class.

3 Read the rubric then play the tape for students to complete the explanations. Let them compare answers in pairs before checking back with you.

> 1 You have to answer the phone immediately.
> 2 You must never sound bored or angry.
> 3 I have to introduce myself to every caller.
> 4 You have to give your name.
> 5 I have to call the customer by name.
> 6 We aren't allowed to end a call without promising to do something.

F

1 Ask students to work in pairs and to carry on explaining the regulations in **E**, using appropriate modals. Let them compare with other pairs before checking back with you.

> **Possible answers:**
> You mustn't have a beard or a moustache.
> You must dress smartly.
> At the end of the day we have to tidy up our desks.
> We aren't allowed to eat or drink in the office.
> We aren't allowed to smoke.
> Breaks must be short.
> You mustn't have personal photos on your desk.
> You are not allowed to receive personal calls.
> We are not really allowed to have days off sick.

As a class, discuss whether these rules are old-fashioned, typical, surprising, etc. Find out about regulations in students' companies. Are there different rules in other countries? As a homework task, students could write out a list of their company / college / school regulations.

2 Ask the class to work in pairs and imagine what changes they would make when taking over a new company, e.g. salary in advance, five hours a day, four-day week, company cars for everyone, etc. Feed back as a class.

G

We are surrounded by signs which tell us what we can and cannot do. Let students work in pairs to say where they would see the signs and what they mean. Check answers with the whole class.

> 1 you can go – at a road junction
> 2 you mustn't go faster than 30 mph – at the roadside
> 3 you must be quiet – in a library
> 4 you must wear a hard hat – on a building site
> 5 you must not smoke – in a restaurant / on a plane
> 6 you can pay by Visa – on a shop door
> 7 you are not allowed in here if you are under 18 – nightclubs / pubs
> 8 you are not allowed to enter here – on a door

Optional extra activity
Ask students to work in pairs and think of other signs, or invent new ones. For each sign they should draw a symbol / picture, and write out a rule. When they have finished, ask them to report back to the class.

10.3 Checking and correcting information

This section deals with a furniture order from the initial enquiry up to the written confirmation.

A

1 In this first activity students have to note down the information from the initial enquiry. Read the rubric, then play the tape twice to ensure they note down all the information correctly. Check answers with the whole class.

> Stephanie Strahl
> Strahl & Sironi
> 13, Ave de Frontenex, CH 1207 Geneva
> 022-787-0540
> send a brochure

Check understanding of the situation by asking some more comprehension questions. Let students clarify and check the information among themselves, e.g.:

– Who wants to buy furniture?	Ms Strahl.
– Who makes the furniture?	A Spanish firm.
– Who sells the furniture?	Laporta.
– What is the next step?	He will send her a brochure.

2 Ask students to read the letter and find the three errors. When they give you the errors, ask them to use a complete sentence. In this way they are practising contrastive stress.

> The company is called Strahl and **S**ironi not **F**ironi.
> The address is **13** not **30** Avenue de Frontenex.
> The postal code is **CH** not **CA**.

3 Ask students to look at the letter again and answer the two questions. Check answers.

> **1** The normal salutation for a woman where you do not wish to refer to her married or unmarried status is *Ms*. Where you start a letter with the name of the person you normally close with *Yours sincerely*.
> **2** a *please find enclosed*   b *a full range*

B

This exercise continues the theme and is a gap-fill based on the language of giving, taking, and checking information.

1 Read the rubric and check understanding of the situation. Ask students to look at the expressions in the box and to use them to complete the dialogue. When they have finished, play the tape so they can check their answers.

> 1 Go ahead
> 2 I didn't catch
> 3 I've got that
> 4 Go on
> 5 Sorry, that's ...
> 6 Have you got that
> 7 Can I read that back to you?
> 8 That's right

Then ask students to read out the dialogue in pairs, using the correct expressions.

2 Ask students to form new pairs and take it in turns to give the information listed. They should use the correct expressions to slow the speaker down, check, clarify, etc. If they need help they can consult the Language Note.

C

1 We have now reached the quotation stage in the process. Ask the class to read the quotation carefully, as they would in real life. Let them work in pairs to answer the questions and then report back to the class.

> 1 a desk and a filing cabinet
> 2 £1,000 + £175 VAT
> 3 whether to have beech or cherry
> 4 confirm in writing

2 This exercise works on contrastive stress, which we use when we correct people. In the Language Note there are two softening expressions, *in fact* and *actually* which will make the exercise sound more natural. Ask students to work in pairs, taking it in turns to read aloud and correct.

> 2 No, she lives in **Geneva**.
> 3 No, she wants to buy some **furniture**.
> 4 No, it's in **Southwark Street**.
> 5 No, it costs £**690**.
> 6 No, it's one metre **eighty**.
> 7 No, it costs £**310**.
> 8 No, it has **two** drawers.

D [74]

Stephanie Strahl still has not ordered her furniture. This listening exercise brings the deal to a conclusion. Before listening, check students understand the questions. Play the tape and then collate answers on the board.

> 1 15%
> 2 Laporta offers a discount on three items (not two).
> 3 Another company does the delivery.
> 4 thirty days after the order
> 5 by e-mail

As a follow-up question, ask who has won the negotiation. Stephanie has got a free chair because she is now paying £1,000 for all four items (before VAT). Antonio manages to sell Stephanie the two items he wanted to sell her. He does not offer a discount on the chair despite offering 15% discount on three items. They both do well – it is a win-win deal.

E

The Laporta–Strahl discussions end with an e-mail confirmation. Ask the class to work in pairs to put it in the correct order. Build up the e-mail on the board.

> The correct order is: 3, 10, 9, 6, 4, 7, 2, 5, 8, 1.

Optional extra activity
Ask students to work in pairs and to think of details of another order between two companies, i.e. they need to change the names, items, and amounts in the Laporta–Strahl order. They can then write an e-mail confirmation of the order.

F

This is a fun activity to end the unit. Read through the rubric and then let students work in pairs to complete the task. Monitor, checking they are stressing corrected information.

> 1 Actually I think it is **eighteen**.
> 2 In fact **Washington** is the capital of the USA.
> 3 No, I think it's 60 **million**, actually.
> 4 No, it isn't. It's a famous **Italian** company.
> 5 No, he doesn't. He lives in **the White** House.

Photocopiable activity (page 76)

This provides further practice in checking information. Ask students to work in pairs.

In **1**, A has to ask most of the questions. In **2**, the roles are reversed. Monitor the exercise carefully, noting good use of language and correcting where necessary. Ask certain pairs to act out the conversation in front of the others.

Unit 11 | Getting a job

11.1 Recruitment processes

A

This exercise introduces the gerund form for talking about personal likes and dislikes. As a warmer, ask students to make a list of good and bad things about their jobs / studies then to report back to the class.

1 Do this as a whole-class activity.

> From left to right:
> I hate / I don't really like / I don't mind / I quite like / I really enjoy

2 Ask students to read the five sentences and find words which mean *computers* (*hardware*), *computer programs* (*software*), *numbers* (*figures*). Then ask them to match the sentences with the pictures. Let them compare answer in pairs before checking back with you.

> **1** d **2** e **3** b **4** a **5** c

3 Do this task with the whole class and refer them to the Language Note. Ask students what else the people in the pictures might say about their jobs, using the same verbs.

> The verb is in the *-ing* form.

4 Give a couple of examples for your own job, then let students work in pairs, using the list of good and bad points they made in **A** for ideas. Students who don't have a job can talk about their studies.

B

1 These extracts from job advertisements contain examples of many of the target adjectives. Let students read the texts individually, then compare answers in pairs. They should be able to guess the job without knowing all the new words. When checking answers, ask them what words in the text gave them the information.

> **Advert A** – sales person
> **Advert B** – computer systems analyst
> **Advert C** – accountant

2 Let students complete this individually, then compare answers in pairs before checking back with you. Ask them to mark the main stress on the adjectives.

If students know each other well, ask them to say which adjectives apply to particular people in the class.

> **1** f **3** h **5** b **7** e **9** i
> **2** a **4** c **6** g **8** j **10** d

3 Refer students to the two model sentences, and point out that an example is given for each quality mentioned. Give two more model sentences of your own. Then let students write their own examples. If possible, let them work in pairs and write about a person they both know. Monitor, checking that students are justifying the qualities mentioned with examples.

C 75a

1 Let students read the initial rubric and the questions. Then play 75a once or twice as necessary, without stopping. Students compare answers before checking back with you.

> **1** Europe, particularly southern Europe, and Southeast Asia
> **2** computer technicians, teachers, construction workers, project managers, engineers (and a personal bodyguard!)
> **3** He specializes in Thailand – he visits companies there and listens to their needs.
> **4** They offer a personalized service to companies, so it's important to get to know the company first.

2 Play 75b once or twice as necessary, without stopping. Let students compare answers, then check with the whole class.

> **He likes:** learning about new cultures, interviewing (young) people, visiting new countries
> **He dislikes:** taking the plane, saying 'no' to candidates who aren't suitable
> **Necessary qualities:** adaptable, sensitive to local culture, outgoing

3 Do this as a whole-class activity. Ask students to give reasons for the adjectives they choose.

> **Possible answers:**
> – independent (because a long way from family)
> – patient (takes a long time to learn the language)
> – good with words (to learn the language quickly)

Teacher's Book   57

D

Start by asking students what kind of information typically goes into an advertisement for a job.

1 Ask students to answer the questions individually. For the question about salary, you will probably need to point out that *K* means *thousand*. Note that salaries are quoted as annual rather than monthly sums.

> 1 European Sales Director for an American company
> 2 yes
> 3 Lyon, France
> 4 qualifications: a degree in Business Administration and preferably another one in Medicine, good level in three European languages including English; experience: 10 years in the medical or pharmaceutical industry, 5 years in management; personal qualities: ambitious, energetic, adaptable
> 5 e-mail a CV and cover letter

2 Encourage students to follow the model advert very closely. You may prefer to start the task in class, then let students finish it for homework.

E

1 Let students complete the chart individually, then compare answers in pairs before reviewing the answers as a class. Check understanding with a few follow-up questions, e.g. *What do you do when you apply for a post?*

> 2 applies for the post
> 4 invites 12 candidates for interview
> 5 attends the interview
> 6 makes a shortlist
> 9 makes a final selection
> 12 resigns from his / her present job

2 Ask students to mark the main stress on each of the words in the box, then to say the words aloud. Let them complete the word-building task in pairs.

Verb	Noun	Person
employ	employment	employer / employee
apply for	application	–
shorlist	short list	–
advertise	advertisement	advertiser
resign	resignation	–

3 Ask students to complete the task individually, then compare answers in pairs. Check answers with the whole class, then ask them to read the sentences aloud to each other, with particular attention to word stress.

> 1 applications
> 2 advertisement
> 3 applicant
> 4 resignation; employer
> 5 shortlisted; interview
> 6 applied; advertise
> 7 employment; resigned

11.2 Applying for a job

A

Introduce the topic by asking students what information should go into: a cover letter; a CV or resume. As a general rule, CVs should contain information about the candidate's education, professional experience, particular skills (including languages), and personal interests; a cover letter should explain his/her motivation for the job, and highlight the qualifications and professional experience particularly relevant to the job applied for.

Refer students back to the job advertisement on page 128. Then ask them to read the covering letter, and discuss Luis Antonio's suitability for the job.

> – He has an MBA and a medical degree.
> – He has many years experience of the pharmaceutical industry (since 1988) and of management (since 1992).
> – He has a good level in two European languages (English and Spanish) and is learning a third. He is also a Portuguese native speaker, being Brazilian.
> – He's ambitious.

B

This activity introduces and practises the past simple / present perfect distinction (only the simple form of the present perfect is introduced in this book).

1 Ask students to discuss Luis's career and complete the time line. Make a copy of the time line on the board, and read through the letter with the students, adding the relevant information to the board as you go along.

82–86	doctor – medical charity in Peru
86–88	MBA course, Los Angeles
88–91	research scientist – Schering Plough
91–92	research scientist – Merck
92–97	in charge of clinical trials – Medilab
99–now	Regional Director for Southern Europe – AVRC

2 Remind students that when we talk about past actions that have no relation to the present, we use the past simple tense. Ask them to complete Luis's first three remarks. Check answers, then draw the following time line on the board to illustrate the concept.

Past simple + *in* or *ago*
in ... ... ago —— NOW

Ask students how they could say Luis's first three remarks in another way, changing the *in* (+ *year*) form to the ... *ago* form and vice versa. Then follow exactly the same procedure for Luis's second three remarks, putting the following time line on the board.

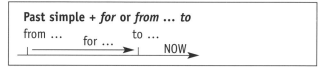
Past simple + *for* or *from ... to*
from ... for ... to ... NOW

Then let students answer the two sets of questions orally with a partner. Elicit answers from the whole class, then write them up on the board next to the relevant time line for students to copy.

Past simple + *in* or *ago*
1 in
2 joined AVRC
3 (count back from present year)
4 He left Peru in 1986 (or x years ago).
5 He resigned from Schering Plough in 1991 (or x years ago).
6 He moved to Europe in 1999 (or x years ago).

Past simple + *for* or *from ... to*
1 for a
2 studied / was
3 for four
4 He worked for Schering Plough for three years (from 1988 to 1991).
5 He was in charge of clinical trials for five years (from 1992 to 1997).
6 He lived in Peru for four years (from 1982 to 1986).

3 Go through the Language Note, then ask students to complete sentences a–c. Let them compare answers in pairs before checking back with you. Illustrate the concept of the present perfect with a time line on the board. Point out that we use *for* both in the past simple and the present perfect but *since* can only be used with the present perfect.

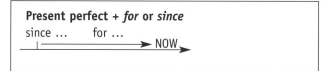
Present perfect + *for* or *since*
since ... for ... —— NOW

Ask students to answer questions d–f orally with a partner. Check answers, writing them on the board next to your time line so students can copy.

1 has been; for
2 has had; since 1988
3 has worked; since
4 He's lived in Europe since 1999 (for x years).
5 He's been Regional Director for Southern Europe since 1999 (for x years).
6 He's worked in the pharmaceutical industry since 1988 (for x years).

Optional extra activity
Ask students to write their own time line for the past twenty years (a shorter time if they are younger), then to work in pairs and ask each other similar past simple and present perfect questions with reference to the time line.

C 76

1 Let students read the rubric. Explain that Luis got to know Bill Pitt some time during his career. It may be useful for them to look at the time line in **B** while listening. Play the tape once or twice as necessary, and give students time to compare answers before checking back with you.

They both did their MBA course at the same time and place (Los Angeles 1986–88).

2 Ask students if they remember any of the details asked for. Then play the tape once or twice more as necessary, giving students time to compare answers before checking back with you. Ask them to write out complete sentences about Bill Pitt, eliciting the first one as an example: *He's worked for Sun Microsystems since 1997.*

Sun Microsystems; 1997
Melissa (Norton); 1991
on MBA course in Los Angeles
San Francisco; 1994

D

1 Refer students to the initial rubric and the first example in the table (*I got married / I've been married*). Point out that the first sentence refers to the ceremony itself – there is no relation to the present, so we use the past simple. In the second sentence we are interested in the state of being married – the person is still married now, so there is a relation to the present, and we use the present perfect. Ask them to complete the missing sentences, then to compare answers with a partner.

Check answers with the whole class, then elicit corresponding questions, e.g. *When did you get married?/ How long have you been married?*

> She's worked for AVRC since 1999.
> They moved here 10 years ago.
> He's known his wife for three years.
> I started this job in January.
> We've been here for an hour.

2 Let students answer these questions orally in pairs. Do a whole-class feedback by asking individual students to report back on their partner.

3 Half the class should look at Students A's information and the other half at File CC on page 155. They should prepare their questions with a partner, then form A / B pairs to ask and answer each other's questions. Monitor, checking for correct use of past simple and present perfect. Then discuss the two follow-up questions with the whole class.

E

Ask students to write their own CV. This could be completed as a homework task. Encourage them to use the CV in **D** as a model.

11.3 Staff profiles

A

Refer students to the cartoon, and discuss the meaning of the term *take early retirement*. Elicit what the advantages of early retirement are for both employer and employee. Are there any disadvantages? Then let students match the phrases, and compare answers with a partner.

| 1 f | 2 e | 3 a | 4 g | 5 d | 6 c | 7 b |

B 77

This exercise introduces the concept of the present perfect for unfinished time (*this year*, *today*, etc.) as contrasted with the past simple for finished time (*last year*, *yesterday*, etc.). It also revises the vocabulary for describing trends.

1 Ask students to read the rubric and look at the table. Remind them of the verbs / verb phrases that go with the nouns in the table, e.g. *redundancies – to be made redundant*. Ask them to work out how many employees the company needs to have at the end of this year to achieve a 10% reduction (600 – 10% = 540). Then play the tape once or twice as necessary, giving students time to compare answers before checking back with you.

	Last year	This year
New employees	60	16
Transfers	4	13
Resignations	5	2
Redundancies	0	6
Dismissals	2	0
Early retirement	6	20
Retirement	7	12
Total at end of year	600	563

No, they haven't achieved their objective.

2 Play the first part of the tape again, stopping after each sentence for students to fill the gaps. Answer the two follow-up questions with the whole class (finished time: past simple; unfinished time: present perfect).

| 1 has fallen | 2 took on | 3 taken | 4 stopped |

3 Look at the two examples together, and elicit the completion of each one. Then let students describe the other changes orally in pairs, before reviewing all the answers with the whole class. Tell the class that the present perfect sentences they have made focus on a slightly different aspect of the tense. Write the following on the board.

> **Present perfect – used to indicate a link between past and present**
> 1) action not finished:
> *I've worked* for my company since 1999.
>
> 2) time of reference not finished:
> *This year* we've taken on sixteen people.

Point out that in the first situation, the person still works for the company; in the second situation the action of taking on sixteen people is finished, but *this year* is not finished. Then ask students to read the Language Note.

Last year ...	This year ...
– they transferred 4 people.	– they have transferred 13.
– 5 people resigned.	– 2 people have resigned.
– they didn't make anybody redundant.	– they've made 6 people redundant.
– they dismissed 2 people.	– they haven't dismissed anybody.
– 6 people took early retirement.	– 20 people have taken early retirement.
– 7 people retired.	– 12 people have retired.

C

This exercise focuses on present perfect questions in the context of unfinished time and shows how we often switch from present perfect when asking about general

60   Teacher's Book

experience to past simple when giving more details.

1 Ask students to do the task individually then compare answers in pairs before checking back with you.

> 1 d   2 c   3 a   4 b

2 Answer these questions as a whole class.

> The questions are in the present perfect, but the answers are principally in the past simple.
> *ever* = 'in your life until now'

3 Divide the class into A / B pairs and refer them to the relevant information. Tell them to use the same combination of tenses in their questions and answers as in **1**. Monitor, asking individual students to self-correct if you hear any grammatical mistakes. As a follow-up, ask students to tell you anything interesting or surprising they learned about their partners.

D

This exercise provides further consolidation of the past simple / present perfect distinction.

1 Answer the first question together. Then give students a minute to study the table. Check understanding by asking a few true / false questions, e.g. *Today, 42% of women prefer a male boss. In 1982, 70% of women had no preference.* Do they find any of the information surprising?

2 Ask students to complete the summary, looking carefully at the time reference in each case before choosing the tense. Point out that more than one answer is possible for some gaps.

> 1 has gone down
> 2 decreased / fell / went down
> 3 has decreased / has fallen / has gone down
> 4 has risen / has gone up / has increased
> 5 preferred
> 6 went up / rose / increased
> 7 has started
> 8 had
> 9 was
> 10 has risen / has increased / has gone up

E [78]

This exercise practises listening for numbers, and provides further discussion on the male / female boss question. Start by asking how this table is different from the previous one (it shows men's opinions). Then play the tape once or twice as necessary, giving students time to compare answers before checking back with you. Answer the final question as a whole class.

> | Male | Female | No preference
> Today | 35 | 12 | 52
> 1993 | 33 | 16 | 49
> 1982 | 40 | 9 | 46
>
> Similarities: the number of men and women who prefer a female boss increased between 1982 and 1993 but has fallen since then.

In a big class with a fairly equal gender mix, you could do a similar survey of their own opinions. Alternatively, they could do a survey of other students or (if in an English-speaking country) of people in the street.

F

This activity can be done individually or in pairs / groups. You could set a 15–20 minute time limit, then see who / which team has the best score.

Photocopiable activity (page 77)
This looks at the subject of motivation at work. Ask students what motivates them to do well in their job. Hand out the questionnaires and ask them to rank the twelve factors in order of importance. The questions help to clarify the meaning of the different terms. Let them compare answers, and reasons for their choice. Feed back, working out a class ranking. If your class all work for companies, or have done so recently, ask them to give their employer a mark out of 10 for each factor. Then compare answers as a whole group or in pairs. Ask them to justify the mark they have given.

Optional follow-up
Students at managerial level may have met different theories on motivation. Frederick Herzberg, in his book *Work and the Nature of Man* (1966) identified two different factors which influence motivation at work:

– 'Motivator' factors: Achievement, Recognition, Job interest, Responsibility, Advancement, Growth. All these increase job satisfaction, and will make an employee want to stay with the company.
– 'Hygiene' factors: Supervision, Company policy, Working conditions, Salary, Peer contact, Security. These do not increase job satisfaction. However, if absent they can create dissatisfaction.

Make lists on the board of 'motivator' and 'hygiene' factors. Explain each term and ask students if they agree with the ideas. Then ask them to total the marks they gave to their company in each category to give two separate scores out of 60. This will indicate the weight their company places on each. Students can then compare the strengths and weaknesses of their companies.

Unit 12 | The world of work

12.1 Changing careers

A

1 Before starting the activity, brainstorm on the board all the words associated with employment that the class knows. A number of the words suggested will appear in the text. Then let students complete the task in pairs. Collate answers on the board and add them to the words produced by the brainstorming session. Check understanding by asking for sentences using the words.

> 1 retire
> 2 be self-employed
> 3 be unemployed
> 4 to be made redundant
> 5 a promotion
> 6 prospects
> 7 an interview
> 8 salary
> 9 a recruitment agency
> 10 a merger

2 Ask the class to read the text in three parts, answering questions 1–5, 6–11, and 12–14. Students have to choose the correct verb form each time. They can work in pairs or individually. The text will generate a lot of discussion and you will not be able to deal with all queries immediately. By the end of the section, however, all the tenses introduced in the book will have been revised.

> 1 started
> 2 retired
> 3 have changed
> 4 work
> 5 are computerized
> 6 I'll take
> 7 has been
> 8 was made
> 9 have written
> 10 I'm going
> 11 will
> 12 is looking
> 13 I'll
> 14 worked

3 This activity checks general understanding of the text and can be done as a whole-class activity with extra comprehension questions added where appropriate. Try to activate the vocabulary introduced in **1**.

> 1 a Sergio b Jürgen, Patricia c Karel
> 2 The prospects were not good and there was little chance of promotion.
> 3 He was made redundant.
> 4 There are too many people in her department since the merger.
> 5 He did not get on with his boss and wanted to be more independent.

B

This exercise clarifies the use of the tense forms introduced in the text.

1 Let students work in pairs to complete the table. Collate answers on the board.

> **Regular repeated actions or situations:** Patricia lives in Madrid.
> **Present actions:** She is looking for another job.
> **Future arrangements:** Next week I'm going to Turin.
> **Predicting:** I think I'll probably leave quite soon.
> **Stating a condition:** If they offer me the job I will take it.
> **Decision:** I'll take it.
> **Finished actions:** I worked for a car company for six years.
> **Unfinished action:** Jürgen has been with the company for the last three years.
> **Unfinished time:** I have written a lot of letters in the last few weeks.
> **Present simple passive:** Many processes are computerized.
> **Past simple passive:** I was made redundant six months ago.

2 In this activity, students have to make questions and answer them, using the various tense forms. Let students work in pairs. Monitor their work and feed back as a class.

> 1 What is Patricia doing? She is looking for another job.
> 2 What does Jürgen do? He works for Lufthansa.
> 3 Where is Sergio going next week? He is going for an interview in Turin.
> 4 How long did Karel work for the car manufacturing company? He worked for them for six years.
> 5 How long has Jürgen worked for Lufthansa? He has worked for them for three years.
> 6 When did Karel start his business? He started his business in 1995.
> 7 What has Sergio written? He has written a lot of letters.
> 8 Where has Patricia registered? She has registered at a recruitment agency.

9 Who is Patricia employed by? She is employed by a pharmaceutical company.
10 When was Sergio made redundant? He was made redundant six months ago.

C 79a

This listening exercise is based on one of the people mentioned in the text, Sergio Laguardia.

1 Ask students to read the rubric then to look at the notes and predict the interviewer's questions – predicting what is going to be said makes comprehension easier. Let them compare answers in pairs.

2 Play 79a once or twice as necessary. Students need to check the questions and listen carefully for Sergio's answers. Feed back as a class referring to the tapescript for answers.

D 79b

This exercise gives students a chance to talk more freely about unemployment and ways of finding a job. It is a situation which most students will have had experience of at some time in their life.

1 Ask students to look at the list of suggestions and comment on them. They can add any advice not given. Feed back as a class.

2 Play 79b for students to complete the task. Let them compare in pairs before checking back with you. The listening passage shows that there are different ways of coping with unemployment. Sergio is only doing two of the things on the list.

5, 7

Optional extra activity
Ask students to work in pairs and to talk about their professional / academic life to date. They can talk about jobs they have had or courses they have done. If they are happy to, they can also talk about any periods of unemployment. If there is time, let them discuss their plans for the future. This activity should result in free practice of all the tenses used in the Student's Book.

E 80a

The section ends with pronunciation and focuses on the stress patterns of some of the long words used in the unit, and on sentence stress.

1 Ask students to read the words quietly to themselves and put them in the correct column. Feed back as a class.

2 Play 80a for students to check answers. Play the tape again and ask them to repeat the words.

ooo●	unemployed
●oo	interview company secretary confident fortunate
o●o	accountant recruitment redundant
ooo●o	information manufactured optimistic
o●oo	psychology responsible
ooo●oo	pharmaceutical psychological

3 Ask students to work in pairs and to make sentences, using as many of the words in **1** as possible. Feed back as a class. Then play 80b as a dictation. Play each sentence twice, once to listen and then for students to write what they hear. Ask different students to write their answers on the board, then correct as a class activity.

12.2 Work environments

A 81

Ask the class to look at the cartoon. Why is it funny? These days more and more people work from home, from airports, on trains, etc. with a wide range of high-tech equipment.

1 Ask students if they ever work away from the office and what equipment they have, etc. Refer students to the rubric and then play the tape so that they can complete the table. The listening passage is quite long so you may need to play it twice to get all the information required.

Rebecca	**Johann**
home	Brussels
very small	very modern open-plan, twenty work-stations
9–3.30 p.m.	7–7 p.m.
quick sandwich	with customers and contacts
TV, fax, phone, PC	computer screens, lap top, phone
pick up children	drink with colleagues

2 Ask students to look at the remarks and see if they can remember who made them. Then play the tape again. Check answers with the whole class.

1 R 2 J 3 R 4 J 5 R 6 R 7 J 8 R 9 R

3 Let students work in pairs to answer the two questions. Feed back as a class.

1 *enough* comes before a noun (*enough data*) but after an adjective (*big enough*).
2 We can put *quantifiers* (*much, many*) and *adjectives* after *too*.

Teacher's Book   63

Language Note
Read through with students before moving on to the next exercise. Check comprehension by eliciting some more examples for each point.

B

This exercise practises *too* and *not enough*.

1 Ask students to complete the task individually, then compare answers in pairs before checking back with you.

> **Possible answers:**
> 1 My salary is too low.
> 2 I don't have enough room.
> 3 She has too much work.
> 4 He wasn't relaxed enough.
> 5 He was too old.
> 6 It doesn't have enough memory.
> 7 His English wasn't good enough.
> 8 He isn't serious enough.

2 This activity lets students use the language in a freer way. Column A is for those who are already working whereas B is better for those who are still studying. Ask the class to work in pairs. You might have language like this:

A
- I travel too much.
- I work too many hours.
- My days aren't long enough for all my work.
- The office isn't big enough; There are too many people in the office.
- I don't have enough responsibility.
- I don't earn enough money in this job.
- My boss is too mean / lazy / nice.

B
- I don't have enough homework.
- My exams were too difficult.
- There are too many people in the class.
- I go out too often.
- My teachers aren't interesting enough.
- My parents don't give me enough money.

3 Ask students to write some sentences about their partner using *too* and *not enough*, and then to report back to the class. Write some examples on the board.

C

This series of activities aims to revise the vocabulary skills covered in the book so far whilst covering the lexical area of computers. Those teachers with limited knowledge of the subject should not worry. Someone in the class will be an expert!

1 Let students do the task individually, then compare answers in pairs before checking back with you.

> **Clockwise from top left:**
> central unit, screen, printer, mouse mat, mouse, keyboard, socket, scanner

2 With the help of the class expert, try to put the actions on to the flow chart. There might be discussion as to whether you go online before you write a message.

> 1 switch on computer   7 connect modem
> 2 open application   8 write e-mail message
> 3 write article   9 attach article
> 4 save document   10 send to editor
> 5 check spelling   11 disconnect modem
> 6 save any changes   12 shut down

Optional extra activity
Ask students to work in pairs and to devise a word chain or flow chart for a process of their choice. Encourage them to use something that has occurred in the Student's Book, e.g. applying for a job. Monitor, giving help where necessary. When they have finished, ask one or two pairs to write their flow chart on the board.

3 This activity focuses on collocations and compounds. Let students work in pairs to complete the task. Feed back as a class. Check understanding by asking them to use the collocations in sentences.

> 1 word-processing; data-base; spreadsheet
> 2 print; open; paste; copy; rename; attach
> 3 paste; copy; print
> 4 open; rename; copy

4 Using word families is another useful skill. Ask students to complete the table and provide an example sentence for each word, to illustrate its meaning.

> **Verb:** scan; connect; computerize
> **Noun:** printer; attachment

5 Example sentences are a good way of recording vocabulary. Ask students to complete the task individually, then compare answers in pairs before checking back with you.

> 2 data base
> 3 attach; attached
> 4 My printer is out of ink.
> 5 We always scan pictures for our newsletter.
> 6 I used a spreadsheet to calculate our prices for next year.

6 The final technique offered is the mind map. Refer students back to page 29, then ask them to create a mind map for computers, including all the vocabulary used in this section. Write an outline mind map on the board and collate answers.

12.3 Saying goodbye

This final section concentrates on reviewing functional language, and teaching the language necessary for concluding business and saying goodbye.

A [82]

This first exercise looks at some 'ending' situations. Ask students to read through the situations. Play the tape so they can match the dialogues to the situations. Check answers with the whole class.

| a 6 | b 5 | c 1 | d 4 | e 2 | f 3 |

B

1 Ask students to work in pairs to complete the four dialogues. Check answers and elicit the nature of each situation:
1 at the end of an interview
2 at the end of a meeting
3 at the end of a visit to someone's house
4 at the end of a phone call

| 1 coming | 3 See | 5 calling | 7 been |
| 2 thank | 4 Thanks | 6 Speak | 8 soon |

2 Now ask students to do the matching task. Let them compare answers in pairs before checking back with you.

| 1 a | 2 c | 3 d | 4 b |

3 Finally, ask students to practise the dialogues in pairs.

C

This exercise gives students plenty of practice in polite goodbyes. Refer them to the Language Note, then ask them to work in pairs to act out the situations. If you like, they can swap partners for each different situation. When they have finished, ask for volunteers to act out their dialogues in front of the class.

Model answers:

A
1 Thanks for a lovely evening.
  You must come to us next time.
  See you soon.
2 That was delicious.
  I'll get the bill.
  Thanks very much.
3 Goodbye then.
  Maybe.

  Thank you. You too.
4 See you tomorrow.

  Oh. Would you like a drink later?
  Seven is fine. See you later.

B
  Thanks for coming.
  Thanks. That would be nice.
  Yes. Bye.
  Yes it was.
  No, this is on me.
  You're welcome.
  See you next year?
  Have a safe journey.
  Thanks. Bye.
  Probably not. I'm on holiday tomorrow.
  That's a good idea. About seven?
  Yes. See you.

D [83a]

1 In this activity students have to respond in a natural way to a prompt on the tape. Most of the language has already featured in the section so it is purely a revision activity. Play [83a] and let students respond to the prompts.

2 Play [83b] for students to listen and compare with their own ideas.

E

This game is intended to revise the language from the whole book. Read through the rubric and check students understand the rules. Demonstrate by throwing a dice and undertaking the task on the square you land on. Then divide the class into teams / pairs to play the game. Monitor, praising good language and asking students to self-correct if you spot any errors.

Possible answers:
1 Hello, I'm ...
2 I'm from Athens.
4 00 335 678 4563
5 I'm a surgeon.
6 77, 78, 79, 80, etc.
7 Could I have a coffee, please?
8 The UK is smaller than the USA.
9 Pleased to meet you.
10 Would you like to go out for dinner?
11 101, 100, 99, 98, etc.
12 I think you should go to the police.
13 No thanks. I'll call back later.

14 Could you say that again, please?
15 Could you call me a taxi, please?
16 I'm sorry but this steak is not cooked enough.
17 Shall I get you an aspirin?
18 Could you tell me the way to the Leaning Tower, please?
19 That's OK.
20 Could I speak to Nathalie Azoulai, please?
21 Thanks for inviting me.
22 Could you speak more slowly, please?
23 Fine thanks.
24 We've been here since yesterday.
25 What are you doing tomorrow?
26 Shall I answer it?
27 Could you hold the line, please?
28 If I see him, I'll tell him.
29 Yes, I am.
30 Did you say 13 or 30?
31 No thanks, I don't smoke.
32 Bye. See you tomorrow.
33 Have you got a single room free?
34 This is on me.
35 Cheers!
36 I'm sorry about that!
37 How far is it from Tokyo to Osaka?
38 How much does a one-way ticket cost from Wellington to Sydney?
39 Could you send me a brochure, please?
40 I've worked here for three years.
41 F, G, H, I, etc.
42 Excuse me. I'm in room X. My bed isn't long enough.
43 Where were you born?
44 How do you say *sauerkraut* in English?
45 I don't think so.
46 Thanks for a lovely evening.
47 Is this seat free?
48 You're welcome.

Photocopiable activity (page 78)

This provides further practice in the vocabulary presented throughout the book. Contestants have to guess a word from the definition given. They have the first letter as a clue. If the answer is an expression they have the first letters of each word, for example PTMY could be 'Pleased to meet you.'

The class should work in groups of three for this game with two candidates and one quizmaster for each group.

One contestant works from top to bottom and one from left to right. They take it in turns to choose a square and hear the definition read by the quizmaster. The aim of the game is to answer seven questions correctly. They must choose touching squares each time. Fill in the completed squares with a different coloured highlighter for each player.

Photocopiable page ①

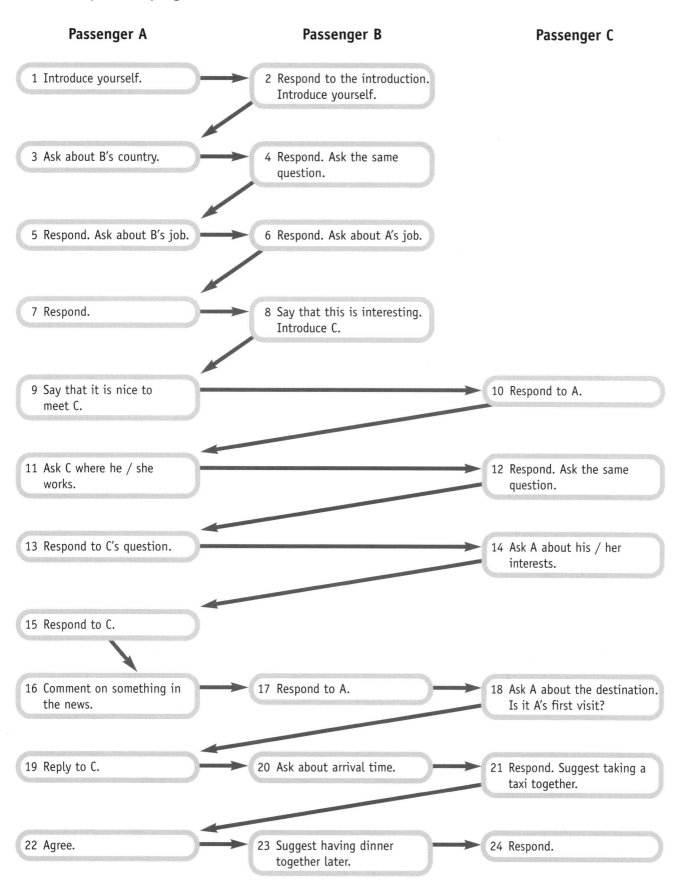

Photocopiable page ②

Student A

① You are a guest at the Novahotel. Your partner is the hotel receptionist. Ask for the following information, using the prompts to help you. Try to continue each conversation.

- Wake-up call – tomorrow morning? (*Could I …?*)
- Shuttle bus to the airport? (*Is there …? What time …? How long …? How much …?*)
- Send an e-mail to the company urgently? (*Could I …? Where …?*)
- Good restaurants near here? (*Are there …? What kind of …? How far …?*)
- Hotel bar? (*Is there …? Where …? What time …?*)

② You are the receptionist at the Imperial Hotel. Your partner is a guest at the hotel and needs some information. Use the information below to help you answer his or her questions. Try to continue each conversation.

ABC Cabs
24-hour service
Telephone: 0098 345 18
standard fare to city centre — $35

```
Bus → city centre – bus stop opposite the hotel
       Dep         Arr
       06.00       06.45
       06.15       07.00
       06.30       07.15
until  22.45       23.30
```

standard luggage allowance 23kgs
hand luggage – 1 piece of hand luggage per passenger

Imperial Hotel

Airport – 40 km   Station – 7 km
Town centre – 10 km

— *Services* —

Fax service available at Reception desk.
Standard charge:
Europe $2 per page
Rest of the world $4 per page

Coin-operated phone by the main entrance at Reception desk.

Credit card phone:
at the entrance to the bar opposite the fitness room on the third floor.

Maps, guides, tourist information available at tourist information centre on first floor.

Student B

① You are the receptionist at the Novahotel. Your partner is a guest at the hotel and needs some information. Use the information below to help you answer his or her questions. Try to continue each conversation.

Shuttle bus
– 24-hour service
Free for hotel guests

Novahotel		airport
06.00	—	06.30
06.30	—	07.00
07.00	—	07.30
07.30	—	08.00

Novahotel
112 East Plantation Avenue

Business Centre (second floor):
Internet and e-mail facilities available 24 hours

Fully equipped Gymnasium and Fitness Centre with heated indoor swimming pool

Bar (first floor):   17.30–22.00
Late Night Bar (basement):
                         23.00–04.00
Hotel Restaurant: 11.30–15.00
                         18.30–23.30

VESUVIA
Fine Italian Cuisine
109 East Plantation Avenue

Banana Joe's Diner
American diner and cabaret restaurant
100 East Plantation Avenue
open all night
Tel: 456-325-455

Thai Orchid
113 East Plantation Avenue
traditional oriental cuisine
Tel 456–323–438

② You are a guest at the Imperial Hotel. Your partner is the hotel receptionist. Ask for the following information, using the prompts to help you. Try to continue each conversation.

- Distance from the hotel to the city centre? (*How far …? Taxi service? How much …? Bus service? How long…?*)
- Credit card phones in the hotel? (*Are there …? Where …?*)
- Street map of the city? (*Have you got / Do you have …? Where can I …?*)
- Hand luggage on the plane? (*How much …?*)
- Send a fax to my company? (*Could I …? How much …?*)

Photocopiable page ③

Caller	Person receiving call
Could I speak to Paul Vidor, please?	Yes, of course. Who's calling, please?
This is Rosa Feron.	Hold on a moment, please.
Hello. Is that Paul?	Yes, speaking.
Hello, Paul. This is Rosa. It's about my visit next week.	Ah yes. Thanks for calling, Rosa. Can I call you back? I'm on another line.
Yes. It's F-E-R-O-N.	Sorry. Could you spell your name, please?
Is Paul in the office today?	No, this is his assistant, Martin Lennon.
Could you ask him to call me back on my mobile?	Yes, he is, but I'm afraid he's at lunch.
Thanks for your help. Goodbye.	Yes, of course. Does he have your number?
OK, I'll hold.	Hello, I'm afraid Paul's in a meeting at the moment.
Yes, I think so. But just in case, it's 0658-4217.	OK. I'll give him the message. Goodbye.
Oh dear. It's quite urgent.	Can I take a message?
Yes, sure. Have you got my mobile number?	Yes, I have. Speak to you in a minute. Bye.

Photocopiable page ④

	Company A	**Company B**	**Company C**	**Company D**
Nationality	Japanese			
Headquarters	Tokyo			
Employees	110,000			
Activity	Electronics			
Sites	Factories in Japan, UK, China, Germany			
Customers	Toyota, Honda, Casio			
Name of company	Panasonic			

✂--

	Company A	**Company B**	**Company C**	**Company D**
Nationality		Swiss		
Headquarters		Emmen, near Lucerne		
Employees		1,800		
Activity		Parts for aviation industry		
Sites		Emmen, Dübendorf, Stans, Zweisimmen, Interlaken, Lodrino, Alpenach		
Customers		Swissair, Airbus, Boeing		
Name of company		SF Emmen		

✂--

	Company A	**Company B**	**Company C**	**Company D**
Nationality			French	
Headquarters			Rueil Malmaison, near Paris	
Employees			1,200	
Activity			Pharmaceuticals	
Sites			Factory and research centre in Orléans	
Customers			Pharmacies, hospitals	
Name of company			Novartis Pharma France S.A.	

✂--

	Company A	**Company B**	**Company C**	**Company D**
Nationality				German
Headquarters				Oberursel
Employees				2,000
Activity				Insurance
Sites				Offices throughout Germany
Customers				General public, companies
Name of company				Alte Leipziger

Photocopiable page 5

Nike sales figures

1 Sales by region: ($ million)

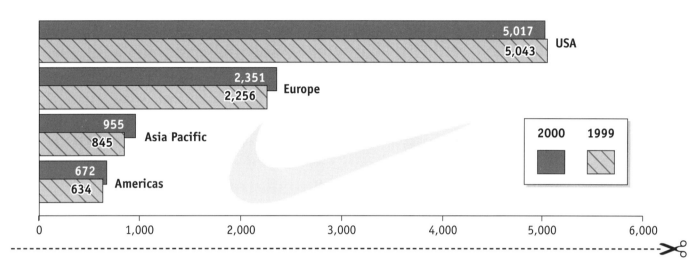

2 Sales by region: percentage of total market

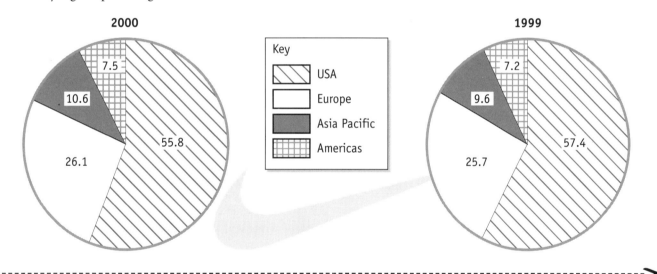

3 Net income ($ million)

	2000	1999
Total sales	8,995	8,777
Gross margin	3,591	3,283
Gross margin %*	39.9	37.4
Net income**	579	451

*Gross margin: profit before tax and other deductions
**Net income: profit after tax

Photocopiable page ⑥

Monday 18 October 2003

9.25 a.m.

Please call Mr Gartner. He will be in town this afternoon. Can he meet you at 2.00 instead of tomorrow morning? Mobile 0779-4562351

Monthly finance meeting
18/10/03 2.00–6.00

1 Monthly results
2 Budget 2004
3 Salary review
4 AOB

Your wife rang! Is it her birthday or something? Did you forget? Call her urgently!

Hi, this is just to say that I will be visiting a colleague on Tuesday 19th. Can I pop in and see you afterwards? If not, how about a drink this evening? I'm at the Four Pillars Hotel until 8.30 a.m. on Tuesday.

Regards, Ken Smith

Memorandum

18 October

To: John Williamson

From: Peter Roberts

I seem to have no monthly results from your department. Please send them to me by 9.30 this morning. This is the second time this year your department has been late with its results. Please telephone my secretary if you have a problem. I look forward to seeing you at today's meeting.

Panaxis Transport →

Dear Sir

We still have no record of payment for Invoice 4536 for $5,600. If we have not received payment by 18 October we will have no choice but to refer the matter to our solicitors.

Yours faithfully

Jacques Grabbe
Financial Director

Photocopiable page 7

Boat Ball

This motorized ball floats on the surface of the water, and has two detachable passenger cabins on each side.

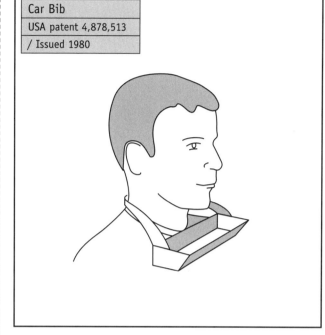

Car Bib

The Car Bib is designed for the motorist who eats while driving, It can also be used as a serving tray for your food.

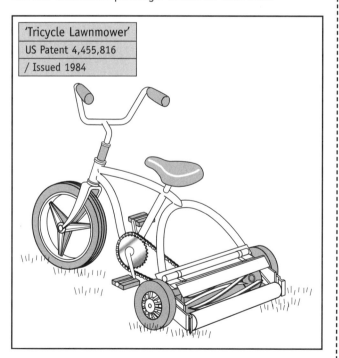

Tricycle Lawnmower

Quieter and cheaper to run than a petrol or electric mower, this tricycle lawnmower protects the environment and gives you lots of useful exercise.

Ski Fan

This gas-powered invention is strapped to your back and steered by hand controls. It can be used for skiing up hills or cross-country.

Photocopiable page ⑧

shares	borrow	bank	sales
expenditure	save	loan	expiry
shareholders	stocks	loss	income
owe	lend	debit	inspector
lose	card	profit	purchase
spend	credit	rise	interest
earn	pay	salary	book
payment	rent	exchange	date
tax	cheque	buy	inflation
rate	account	sell	investment

Photocopiable page 9

Student A

Complaints

- Excuse me. It's very cold here by the window.
- Excuse me. I think you gave me the wrong change.
- Hello again. I'm afraid I can't find the car. You did say bay 225?
- Excuse me, but your phone doesn't accept my credit card.
- But I wanted a seat in non-smoking!

Responses

- I'm sorry about that. I'll send someone upstairs to look at it.
- Oh, no! I picked up the old one by mistake!
- Sorry, sir, but there's nothing I can do about the traffic.
- Sorry to hear that. Could I see your luggage receipt, please?
- I do apologize, madam, but all gentlemen are required to wear a shirt and tie.

✂ ---

Student B

Complaints

- Excuse me. The shower isn't working in my room.
- Could you possibly drive a little faster? My train leaves in fifteen minutes.
- I'm afraid this passport isn't valid, sir. It expired three months ago.
- Excuse me, but that man at the door is my husband.
- Hello. My suitcase wasn't on the carousel.

Responses

- I'm sorry about that, madam. Would you like to move to another table?
- No, sir. I'm afraid that one only takes phone cards.
- I'm very sorry, but they're all taken.
- Yes, on the second underground level of the car park, sir.
- I'm sorry about that. I thought you gave me a $20 note.

© Oxford University Press

Photocopiable page ⑩

Student A

1

You are on a trip to Paris. You have to meet a colleague arriving today. Telephone him or her and obtain and / or check the following information.

- Check that you are speaking to B.
- Confirm the arrival time.
- Check which airport B is arriving at.
- Check the flight number.
- Check the airline: British Airways or British Midland?
- Check the hotel – same as yours? (Hotel Solferino, rue de Lille)
- Ask the best way of getting to the city centre. (bus or taxi?)
- Arrange a meeting place for dinner.
- Find out the nearest metro station.
- Confirm that the table is booked.
- End the conversation.

2

You work in the Sales department of JTB, a company based in Dundee in Scotland. Your boss is the Sales Director Lindsey McPherson. You receive a telephone call.

- Confirm your identity.
- Greet the caller.
- Confirm the time of the appointment. (tomorrow at 10.00 a.m.)
- Lindsey McPherson will be at the meeting with Matthew McLaren the Finance Director. Thomas McCartney is sick.
- JTB is in Princess St.
- It's ten minutes walk from the station.
- JTB have asked for the meeting to discuss a large new order.
- Note his mobile number.
- End the conversation.

Student B

1

You are on a trip to Paris. You have to meet a colleague arriving today. He / she telephones you to get / check the following information.

- Confirm your identity.
- You are arriving at 13.50.
- You are landing at Charles de Gaulle airport.
- Your flight number is BD 170.
- It's a British Midland flight.
- You are staying at a hotel in rue de Lille.
- You think the train is the best way to the city centre.
- You would like to meet at the Alcazar in rue Mazarine.
- Odéon is the nearest metro station.
- You haven't booked a table. Ask your colleague to do that because you are still in London.
- End the conversation.

2

You are in Scotland on business. You are in your hotel and want to check some details about your next appointment. You telephone and talk to a secretary in the Sales department.

- Check you are speaking to Lindsey McPherson's secretary.
- Introduce yourself.
- Confirm the time of the appointment. (tomorrow at 10.30 a.m.)
- Check the names of the people coming. (Lindsey McPherson and Thomas McCartney)
- Confirm the address of JTB.
- Find out if you should walk or take a taxi from the station.
- Confirm the reason for the meeting. (prices for next year)
- Offer your mobile number if there is a problem. (0779–84523)
- End the conversation.

Motivation and Satisfaction

What motivates you in your job? Rank the following factors from 1 (not important) to 12 (very important). Then give your company a mark out of 10 for each factor.

ACHIEVEMENT	Are the objectives of your job clear? Do you think that your job has a real importance to the company and / or to society?	☐	☐
SECURITY	Do you think that your position in the company is safe, i.e. that you will still have a job one or two years from now?	☐	☐
PEER CONTACT	Do you have a good relationship with your colleagues?	☐	☐
SALARY	Are you well paid for the job that you do?	☐	☐
RECOGNITION	Do your superiors often tell you they are pleased with the work that you do?	☐	☐
JOB INTEREST	How interesting is the work that you do?	☐	☐
RESPONSIBILITY	How much freedom do you have to make your own decisions or to manage the work of employees in your team?	☐	☐
SUPERVISION	Does your boss give you lots of helpful advice?	☐	☐
WORKING CONDITIONS	Are you generally happy with your work environment, working hours, and the quantity of work you are given?	☐	☐
ADVANCEMENT	Is it easy for ambitious employees to move to a higher position in the company?	☐	☐
COMPANY POLICY	Are you happy with your company's business strategy?	☐	☐
PERSONAL GROWTH	Are you learning new skills in your job? Does it become more interesting as time goes by?	☐	☐

Photocopiable page ⑫

A	SYL	*H*	**M**	*T*	HB	B	*D*	**B&B**	*C*
E	*I*	K	BF	*L*	**P**	*G*	TVM	HD YD?	*S*
WAYF?	*O*	*M*	**J**	*D*	HAY?	P&L	*F*	**GM**	*R*
E	*N*	WIYN?	*C*	*V*	**P**	*T*	CC	CIHY?	*TF YH*

✂--

Definitions

A	list of points to be discussed at a meeting **AGENDA**	J	going from one place to another **JOURNEY**
B & B	type of British guesthouse **BED AND BREAKFAST**	K	the part of the computer you use to type words and numbers **KEYBOARD**
BF	to change the date of an appointment to an earlier time or date **BRING FORWARD**	L	an apparatus in a building that carries you from one floor to another **LIFT**
B	a commercial name used by a company for itself or its products **BRAND**	M	to change your home or business address **MOVE**
C	the amount you pay for something **COST**	M	a printed list of things to eat in a restaurant or hotel **MENU**
C	a company which is active in the same market as your company **COMPETITOR**	N	verb meaning to see or to observe **NOTICE**
CC	plastic money **CREDIT CARD**	O	place where people work **OFFICE**
CIHY?	offer to be of assistance **CAN I HELP YOU?**	P	to output a copy onto paper **PRINT**
D	an organized list of information (names, addresses, etc.) on a computer **DATABASE**	P	another name for Human Resources **PERSONNEL**
D	part of a company which has a particular function **DEPARTMENT**	P & L	description of a company's financial results **PROFIT AND LOSS**
E	opposite of late **EARLY**	R	a group of products sold by one company **RANGE**
E	to receive money for work **EARN**	S	not dangerous **SAFE**
F	a building with machines where goods are made **FACTORY**	SYL	expression used to someone you will see later in the day **SEE YOU LATER**
G	somebody staying in a hotel **GUEST**	T	a general direction or tendency **TREND**
GM	greeting made before midday **GOOD MORNING**	T	the total sales of a company **TURNOVER**
H	to pay money for something or someone for a short time **HIRE**	TFYH	expression used when someone has given you assistance **THANKS FOR YOUR HELP**
HAY?	informal question when you meet someone **HOW ARE YOU?**	TVM	common expression of gratitude **THANKS VERY MUCH**
HB	greeting to someone on a special day **HAPPY BIRTHDAY**	V	an opinion about something **VIEW**
HDYD?	formal greeting when you meet somebody for the first time **HOW DO YOU DO?**	WAYF?	question asked about someone's nationality **WHERE ARE YOU FROM?**
I	verb meaning to go up **INCREASE**	WIYN?	common introductory question **WHAT IS YOUR NAME?**

Progress test 1 (Units 1–3)   100 marks

A You and your company
(12 marks)

Choose the correct verbs to complete this conversation, as in the example.

A: Where *do / are* you from, Anton?
B: I *'m / be* [1] from Milan, in Italy. And you?
A: I *comes / come* [2] from Jakarta, in Indonesia.
B: Oh, really? And who *do / does* [3] you work for?
A: I *don't / doesn't* [4] work for a company. My husband and I *has / have* [5] an export business.
B: And what do you *export / exports* [6]?
A: Local hand-made products – furniture, ornaments, things like that.
B: That's interesting. So *does / is* [7] your company based in Jakarta?
A: Yes, it is. But we *don't / aren't* [8] there very often. My husband *travel / travels* [9] a lot in Europe, and I *work / works* [10] more in North America.
B: So he *don't / doesn't* [11] see you very often!
A: No. But we *are / do* [12] usually at home in July and August.

B Asking questions
(12 marks)

Put the words in the right order to make questions as in the example.

1 is name your What ?
 ..*what is your name?*..

2 work do you for Who ?
 ....

3 turnover What company's the annual is ?
 ....

4 hotel many in rooms are How the there ?
 ....

5 name and Could give telephone your number me you?
 ....

6 time train the does next leave What ?
 ....

7 there a to Is this plane Tokyo afternoon ?
 ....

C Numbers
(11 marks)

Match the numbers on the left (1–8) with those on the right (a–h), as in the example.

1 194   a quarter past nine in the evening
2 9.45 a.m.   b one thousand, nine hundred and forty-five
3 1945   c quarter to eight in the evening
4 9.15 p.m.   d nine hundred and forty-five dollars
5 £94.50   e one hundred and ninety-four
6 1,945   f nineteen forty-five
7 19.45   g nine forty-five in the morning
8 $945   h ninety-four pounds fifty

Now write these numbers in words.
Example: 256   *two hundred and fifty-six*

9   1998   ....
10   e132.70   ....
11   10.30 a.m.   ....
12   78,340   ....

D Prepositions
(10 marks)

Choose the correct preposition: *on, at, in, by, from, to,* or *opposite*, as in the example.

> **Hotel Restaurants**
>
> The *Salad House* restaurant is located ...*on*... the ground floor, just next .... [1] reception. It is open .... [2] 11.00 a.m. .... [3] 2.30 p.m., seven days a week.
>
> The *Buffalo Bill Steak Bar* is just .... [4] the main entrance to the hotel, ... [5] Queen Street. .... [6] Tuesdays and Thursdays, enjoy your meal while listening .... [7] the sweet sounds of our in-house jazz pianist, Sammy Roe. The music starts .... [8] 12.00 midday.
>
> To reserve a table in advance, please go .... [9] reception. Payment is possible .... [10] cheque and all major credit cards.

E Too many words

(10 marks)

There is one word too many in each of these sentences. Which word is it?

Example: *He's is a sales manager.*

1. Do are there any hotels near here?
2. Where do you are live?
3. My company is produces medical equipment.
4. Can I to speak to Mrs Forster, please?
5. I often go for cycling at weekends.
6. He doesn't have got a car.
7. Do would you like to have dinner with me tonight?
8. How much bottles wine do we need to buy?
9. Come at seven o'clock, and we'll eat at half-past to seven.
10. I would like playing tennis at weekends.

F Travelling

(19 marks)

Look at the mini-dialogues, and complete each space with a word from the box, as in the example.

course	lounge	ticket	employ
hold	key	factory	safe
control	head	starter	bill
based	shower	check in	speak
single	receipt	message	dessert

On the phone

1
A: Could I ...*speak*... to Xavier, please?
B: Yes. .... the line one moment – I'll just call him.

2
A: Can I take a .... ?
B: No, that's OK. I'll call back later.

In a restaurant

3
A: Would you like a .... ?
B: No, just a main .... And maybe a .... after that.

4
A: Here's your .... , sir. How would you like to pay?
B: By credit card. And could I have a .... , please?

In a hotel

5
A: So, that's a .... room, with ....
B: Yes, that's right. For two nights.

6
A: Here's your .... Your room is on the first floor.
B: Thank you. Is there a .... in the room for my valuables?

In a company

7
A: Is this the .... office?
B: No, we're .... in Ankara.

8
A: How many people do you .... here?
B: Thirty-five, and another 150 in the new ....

In an airport

9
A: Is this the .... desk for Milan?
B: Yes. Could I see your .... and passport, please?

10
A: Excuse me. Where's the departure .... ?
B: Just go through passport .... , and you'll see it, sir

G Social exchanges

(8 marks)

Match a Person A sentence (1–8) with a Person B response (a–h) to make eight mini-dialogues.

Person A

1. Could I borrow your newspaper? ....
2. Can he call me back next Monday? ....
3. Would you like something else to drink? ....
4. Would you like to come for dinner? ....
5. May I smoke? ....
6. I'd like the chicken salad, please. ....
7. Excuse me. ....
8. Could I leave half an hour early? ....

Person B

a I'm afraid not. It's not possible here.
b Yes, of course. I'll ask him to do that.
c Certainly. And for you, madam?
d I'm sorry, but we're very busy.
e That would be very nice.
f Yes, of course. Here you are.
g No, thanks. One's enough for me.
h Yes?

80 Progress Tests

H Short answers
(10 marks)

Answer these questions with information about yourself. Give short answers of three words, beginning with *Yes* or *No* as in the example.

1 Are you English ..*No, I'm not*..

2 Is your teacher English?
   ....

3 Does your teacher speak your language?
   ....

4 Are you a student?
   ....

5 Do you work for a company?
   ....

6 Is the town where you live very big?
   ....

7 Are there many museums in your town?
   ....

8 Is there a river in the centre of town?
   ....

9 Do you like speaking English?
   ....

10 Would you like to live in an English-speaking country?
   ....

11 Do you have any English friends?
   ....

I Being polite
(8 marks)

Read this dialogue in a railway station. Choose the most appropriate word or phrase to complete the dialogue.

A: *Excuse me / Please / Pardon* [1], I need some information.
B: Yes, sir. How can I help you?
A: *I like / I'd like / I will* [2] to know about train times to London.
B: *Go ahead / Not at all / Of course* [3], sir. When *would / do / are* [4] you like to travel?
A: First thing tomorrow. *Can / Do / Let's* [5] I get a train before eight in the morning?
B: Let me see. No, I'm *sorry / afraid / see* [6] the first train is at 8.30 on a Sunday. The next one's at 9.45.
A: OK, thanks. *May / Could / Do* [7] you give me a single ticket for the 8.30 train?
B: I'm *afraid / sorry / can* [8] not, sir. This office is just for information. The ticket counter is just next door.
A: OK. Thanks for your help.
B: You're welcome.

Progress test 2 (Units 4–6) 100 marks

A A business trip
(10 marks)

Choose the correct form of the verb to complete this report, as in the example.

> Oxford, Wednesday, 11 September
> I <u>arrived</u> / arrive¹ here last Sunday after a long flight from Thailand. I *leaved* / *left*² Bangkok at midday. I *taked* / *took*³ the bus from Heathrow to Oxford. I *get* / *got*⁴ to the hotel in time for dinner. I *stay* / *am staying*⁵ at the Randolph Hotel. On Monday I *am visiting* / *visited*⁶ a factory in Manchester. I *went* / *goed*⁷ there by train. Tomorrow I *am going* / *going*⁸ to Cardiff to attend a conference. At the weekend I *fly* / *am flying*⁹ to Munich for the International Computer Fair. Next Tuesday I *am seeing* / *saw*¹⁰ Jack Thompson who I *meet* / *met*¹¹ in Tokyo last year at the MicroMac Trade Fair.

B Times and dates
(8 marks)

It is now 9.00 a.m. on Wednesday, 11th September. Write the correct time, day, or date to answer these questions, as in the example.

1 What was the date yesterday? *10th September*
2 What is the date tomorrow? ....
3 What day is it tomorrow? ....
4 What is the time in one hour and a half? ....
5 What was the date one week ago? ....
6 What was last month? ....
7 What is next month? ....
8 I am leaving in two hours. What time am I leaving? ....
9 What was the time fifteen minutes ago? ....

C Vocabulary check
(17 marks)

Complete each sentence with a word or phrase from the box, as in the example.

manufacture	competitors	accounts	advertise
Division	customer	product	production
training	factory	recruit	employs
turnover	employees	suppliers	Purchasing
subsidiaries	parent company		

1 The company ..*employs*.. about 10,000 people.
2 They .... televisions at their .... in Scotland.
3 Last year the .... was £26 million with profits of £2 million.
4 They plan to .... new personnel for the Sales Department.
5 In January they are launching a new ....
6 There are nearly 150 .... in the Marketing ....
7 At the end of the year the .... of the company are audited.
8 Their biggest .... is ELF, which buys 60% of their total ....
9 Tricon Global Restaurants is the .... of Pizza Hut. KFC and Taco Bell are two other .... in the group.
10 Virgin Airlines is one of British Airways main ....
11 They .... on TV and in newspapers.
12 The .... manager organizes courses for the staff.
13 The .... Department is responsible for buying raw materials.
14 We use local .... for all our raw materials.

D Asking questions
(10 marks)

Put the questions in the right form to complete this conversation, as in the example.

A: Hello, Mireille. (How / be / you) ..*How are you?*..¹
B: Fine thanks, Martin. I called you last week, but you were away. (Where / be / you) ² .... ?

82 Progress Tests

A: I was in Prague.
B: Oh, really? (Where / you / stay) ³ .... ?
A: At the Hilton. (Know / you / Prague) ⁴ .... ?
B: Yes, I do. My daughter is working there at the moment.
A: Oh, really? (What / she / do there) ⁵ .... ?
B: She's working for Chanel. Just for one year.
A: (What / do / you) ⁶ .... here today?
B: I'm meeting a customer this afternoon. (Know / you / Peter Gordon) ⁷ .... ?
A: I don't think so. (What / he / do) ⁸ .... ?
B: He's an accountant with Cooper's.
A: Right. So, (when / you / arrive) ⁹ .... ?
B: I came yesterday. By Eurostar. (What / you / do) ¹⁰ .... this evening?
A: Nothing special. (Like / you / eat out) ¹¹ .... somewhere?
B: That would be great.

E Social exchanges

(10 marks)

Match each question (1–10) with a reply (a–j).

1 Would you like a coffee?
2 How's business?
3 How was your flight?
4 My wife is not very well.
5 How do you do?
6 When is your birthday?
7 Can we meet next Monday?
8 See you next week, then.
9 Cigarette?
10 Could I speak to Siobhan Peters?

a Sorry, I'm busy that day.
b Great. I look forward to it.
c It's on November 23rd.
d Speaking.
e No, thank you. I don't smoke.
f How do you do?
g Yes, please, white with no sugar.
h A bit long. Thanks for meeting me.
i Fine.
j I'm sorry to hear that.

F Trends

(10 marks)

Contradict these sentences, as in the example.

1 Prices are going up.
   No, they aren't. They're going down.
2 Life expectancy is decreasing.
   ....
3 Sales fell last year.
   ....
4 Exports are rising at the moment.
   ....
5 The number of users went down in March.
   ....
6 Our turnover fell by 2% in 2001.
   ....

G Missing words

(9 marks)

There is a word missing from each of these sentences. Rewrite each sentence including the missing word.
Example: Where you go last week?
         Where **did** you go last week?

1 I afraid he's not here this afternoon.
   ....
2 My boss travelling to the Czech Republic on Thursday.
   ....
3 I arrived on Saturday six o'clock.
   ....
4 She's research scientist with Roche.
   ....
5 There two secretaries in this department.
   ....
6 I work very hard so in evening I like to relax.
   ....
7 I'd like to speak Mr Taylor, please.
   ....
8 How are you staying? Just three days?
   ....
9 I usually have lunch between one two o'clock.
   ....

H Prepositions

(10 marks)

Complete these dialogues with the correct preposition: *at, after, on, to, in, by, for,* or *about*.

Dialogue 1
A: So, ... Monday I'm flying .... Munich.
B: What time are you leaving?
A: .... six.
B: And how long are you staying?
A: .... two days.

Dialogue 2

C: How .... Friday for our next meeting?
D: Sorry, I'm away that day. Can you manage Thursday?
C: Yes, but I prefer .... lunch.
D: I'm afraid I'm busy .... the afternoon.

Dialogue 3

E: Shall we go then?
F: Yes. How are we getting .... the company?
E: .... car. It's .... the car park.

I Telephone talk

(8 marks)

Put this telephone conversation in the right order, as in the example.

- ☐ I'm afraid he's not here today.
- ☐ Thank you for calling. Goodbye.
- ☐ Then could you put me through to his assistant, Tamsin Rossiter?
- ☐ OK, I'll call back tomorrow.
- ☑ PCS. Good morning.
- ☐ I'm afraid her line's busy. Can I take a message?
- ☐ No, that's OK, thanks. When is Mr Farrar due back?
- ☐ Could I speak to Bill Farrar, please?
- ☐ Tomorrow morning, I think.

J Confusing words

(8 marks)

Choose the correct word to complete each sentence about Maeva Berson and her employer, FTP Atlantique, as in the example.

1 Maeva Berson *is* / *has* thirty-five.
2 She *stays* / *lives* about twenty kilometres from Brest.
3 Her *travel* / *journey* to work takes about thirty minutes.
4 She *takes* / *has* lunch between 12.30 and 1.30.
5 She sometimes *travels* / *works* to Paris for meetings.
6 She *spends* / *passes* her holidays in Italy or Greece.
7 She *assists* / *attends* two or three meetings every week.
8 Most of her *customs* / *customers* are in Brittany.
9 The company employs about 200 *persons* / *people*.

Progress test 3 (Units 7–9) 100 marks

A Comparatives and superlatives
(13 marks)

Look at this interview between a TV journalist and someone who travels a lot by plane. Complete the sentences using the correct form of the adjective, as in the example.

A: Welcome to Heathrow Airport, the (large) *largest* airport in Britain. With me is someone who comes here often. Michael Flinders is one of British Airways' (frequent) .... ¹ flyers. Michael, welcome.
B: Thank you.
A: So, Michael, you came here by train today. Which do you prefer, travelling by plane or by train?
B: Flying is much (nice) .... ² than going by train. It's (fast) .... ³, (clean) .... ⁴ and (cheap), ... ⁵.
A: And what is your favourite airline?
B: I think Singapore Airlines has the (good) .... ⁶ food of all the airlines and the (friendly) .... ⁷ cabin crew.
A: And is flying safe, in your opinion?
B: Oh, yes. It is (dangerous) .... ⁸ to drive on a motorway than to take a plane.
A: Are there any disadvantages to flying?
B: Well, one problem is the food. It's not usually (good) .... ⁹ as on the ground! One of the (bad) .... ¹⁰ meals of my life was on a flight from Budapest to Paris. But overall, I think flying is the (good) .... ¹¹ way to travel and the (convenient) .... ¹². The (big) .... ¹³ problem is getting to the airport!

B Past events
(8 marks)

Complete the sentences with an appropriate past tense form of the verb in brackets.

Example: The company (create) *was created* in 1955.
He (open) *opened* his first restaurant in Illinois.

1 Ford Motors (found) .... in 1903.
2 Prince Alwaleed bin Talal (study) .... in San Francisco.
3 In 1935 PanAm (start) .... flights to Asia.
4 The Big Mac™ (introduce) .... in 1968.
5 The first Levi jeans (make) .... for cowboys and gold prospectors.
6 AOL (acquire) .... Time Warner in 2000.
7 Bill Clinton (win) .... two Presidential elections.
8 The Eiffel Tower (build) .... to celebrate the 100th anniversary of the French Revolution.

C Question formation
(14 marks)

Put the words in the right order to make questions.

1 born When he was ?
   ....
2 the did Why cancel meeting they ?
   ....
3 problem you look the Could into ?
   ....
4 week doing you What next are ?
   ....
5 you full if do hotel the What is will ?
   ....
6 the the in What longest is bridge world ?
   ....
7 factory they Why building are new a ?
   ....
8 town is in What best restaurant the the ?
   ....
9 much weigh How it does ?
   ....
10 founded company was the When ?
    ....
11 copy you Shall send I another ?
    ....
12 back you Can me call ?
    ....
13 is view on What this your ?
    ....
14 Paris to travel What best is way the to?
    ....

D Word partners
(15 marks)

Find pairs of words in boxes A and B that correspond to the definitions below, as in the example.

A

radio	relaxing	acquire	fast
interesting	general	business	long
easy	safe	create	expand
weigh	shopping	department	direct

B

weight	slow	public	boring
difficult	adverts	dangerous	acquisition
stressful	expansion	centre	store
mailing	short	creation	people

1 Two types of sales outlet.

   department   *store*

   ....

2 Six adjectives and their opposites.

   ....
   ....
   ....
   ....
   ....
   ....

3 Four verbs from A and their corresponding noun forms from B.

   ....
   ....
   ....
   ....

4 Two types of advertising.

   ....

5 Two types of customer.

   ....

E Social exchanges
(10 marks)

Match each statement or question (1–10) with a reply (a–j).

1 We never received your brochure.
2 I'm afraid this flight is fully booked.
3 What's it used for?
4 Can someone answer the telephone?
5 How do you feel about this, Cristelle?
6 I'm leaving now.
7 Shall I call you back?
8 This isn't my room key.
9 What are your plans for next week?
10 Mr Bell is late again.

a I think I'll go, too.
b I'll get it.
c I do apologize.
d Shall I call him on his mobile?
e Sorry about that. I'll send you another one.
f I'm finishing the sales report.
g I disagree.
h Yes, please, in about five minutes.
i It's for downloading files.
j OK, I'll take the next one.

F Missing words
(10 marks)

There is a word missing from each of these sentences. Rewrite each sentence including the missing word.

Example: My holiday was expensive than last year.
          *My holiday was **more** expensive than last year.*

1 I think it rain later today.

   ....

2 The restaurant is full, I afraid. Would you like to eat later?

   ....

3 Sparkling wine is not expensive as champagne.

   ....

4 Ms Lingwood arrived ten minutes.

   ....

5 If you advertise, I think you will sell lot.

   ....

6 I call you back tomorrow morning.

   ....

7 Wimbledon is most famous tennis tournament in the world.

   ....

8 I'm very sorry that.
    ....

9 We'll be late we don't leave now.
    ....

10 I look forward meeting you next week.
    ....

G Describing products
(12 marks)

Complete these descriptions of products with words from the box. Then decide what product is being described.

square	rectangular	round	thick
video-cassette	wide	weighs	clear
plastic	compact disc	about	black

Product 1
It is used for storing digital data or music. It is .... ¹, about 12 cm in diameter. It's made of .... ². It is only about 1mm .... ³, and it has a 1cm hole in the centre. It often has a .... ⁴ case made of .... ⁵ plastic.
It is a .... ⁶.

Product 2
It is used for recording from the TV. It is .... ⁷, 20 cm long by 10 cm .... ⁸. It is .... ⁹ 2.5cm thick and .... ¹⁰ about 250 grammes. It is usually .... ¹¹ in colour and comes in a box.
It is a .... ¹².

H Time expressions
(9 marks)

Look at this list of key dates in the history of Williams Grand Prix Engineering.

1968	Frank Williams founds the company.
1979	First victory for Williams in a Grand Prix.
1980	Alan Jones becomes World Champion in a Williams car.
1986	Frank Williams has a car crash in France.
1993	Williams' top driver, Ayrton Senna, dies at Imola.

Now complete these sentences. Put the verb in the right form.

1 Frank Williams .... the company .... years ago.
2 They .... their first Grand Prix over twenty years ....
3 The .... year, Alan Jones .... World Champion.
4 In 1986, Frank Williams .... a car crash in France.
5 Ayrton Senna .... years ago.

I Financial vocabulary
(9 marks)

Complete each sentence with a word or phrase from the box, as in the example.

| profit | loss | lend | borrow | save |
| customers | salary | shares | loan | interest rate |

1 Banks *lend* money to their ....
2 The .... is repaid over a fixed period of time.
3 The .... at the moment is 6%.
4 The average .... in the UK in 1998 was £18,000 per year.
5 If a company spends more than it earns, it makes a ....
6 If you want to .... money, you can put it in a deposit account.
7 If you buy something for £100 and sell it for £150, you make a ....
8 You can buy and sell .... on the Stock Exchange.
9 To buy a house you usually need to .... money from a bank.

Progress test 4   (Units 10–12)   100 marks

A Suggesting

(10 marks)

Choose the correct word or words to complete this conversation between a Sales Manager (B) and his boss (A).

A: Sales for last month were down again. What *are / do / can* ¹ you think we should do?

B: Well, I think we should *employing / to employ / employ* ² another salesperson. I just don't have enough people to cover all the country.

A: I'm sorry, but I *'m not / don't / not* ³ agree. You have a team of eight people now. That's three more than last year.

B: Then why *not / don't / do* ⁴ we increase our discount to our best customers? There's a lot of competition on price, you know.

A: No, I *think / do think / don't think* ⁵ we *should / shouldn't / don't* ⁶ do that. Our prices are too low already – we *can't / don't have to / don't* ⁷ reduce them again. No, I think we *don't have to / must / mustn't* ⁸ get better results from your sales team.

B: How about *offer / to offer / offering* ⁹ them a performance bonus if they increase sales by a certain amount?

A: No, that's just not possible. I'm afraid there's only one solution – you'll *have to / must / can* ¹⁰ start looking for another job!

B Talking about the past

(12 marks)

Rewrite these sentences without changing the meaning, using the words in brackets.

Examples: I've been married for eight years. (get / ago)
            I got married eight years ago.

            I bought my car six months ago. (have / for)
            I've had my car for six months.

1 They've lived here for twenty years. (move / ago)

   ....

2 I joined my company in 1997. (work / for)

   ....

3 I've been Sales Director since 1996. (become / ago)

   ....

4 He arrived here two days ago. (be / for)

   ....

5 She got this job two years ago. (have / for)

   ....

6 We've had this business since 1998. (start / in)

   ....

C Job applications

(10 marks)

Complete this letter of application for a job. The first letters of each word are given.

> Dear Sir / Madam
>
> I am writing in response to your ....ad...¹ in last Sunday's *Observer* newspaper, in which you ask for ene............ ² and amb............ ³ young engineers with a desire to learn.
>
> As you can see from my enclosed CV, my present employer is Millbank Foods in Cambridge. I je............ ⁴ the company five years ago, and I now manage a team of five technicians. This pe............ ⁵ has given me useful work exp............ ⁶, but there is little opportunity for further professional development. That is why I have decided to ap............ ⁷ for the advertised post.
>
> If you would like to discuss my appl............ ⁸, I would be very pleased to come for an in............ ⁹. I look forward to he............ ¹⁰ from you.
>
> Yours faithfully
>
> Timothy Pilkington

88   Progress Tests

D Company rules

(13 marks)

Look at the company rules for Brigitte's new job. Then complete the conversation with words or phrases from the box. You can use each word or phrase more than once.

Company rules
- Flexible working hours: 8 hours chosen between 7.00 a.m. and 8.00 p.m.
- Smoking room on ground floor – no smoking in office
- Work one Saturday per month

| can | allowed | enjoy | mind |
| have to | don't have to | hate | |

A: Hi, Brigitte. How's the new job going?
B: Very well, thanks. I really .... [1] the work.
A: Do you .... [2] start early in the morning?
B: No, I don't. I'm very pleased about that, because I .... [3] getting up early. I .... [4] start when I want. It's a flexitime system. I just .... [5] work a total of eight hours between 7.00 a.m. and 8.00 p.m., that's all.
A: That's nice. .... [6] you smoke in your new office, or do you .... [7] go outside?
B: I'm not .... [8] to smoke in my office, but there's a special smoking room where I .... [9] have a cigarette. I don't .... [10] doing that, because I smoke less now.
A: Yes, it's much better for your health. And is the office very busy?
B: Yes, very. In fact I .... [11] work one Saturday in four to do the end of month accounts. That's the one disadvantage. I don't really .... [12] working at weekends, but that's part of the job.
A: And you .... [13] work every Saturday.
B: No, I don't. That's true. One Saturday per month isn't bad.

E Checking information

(9 marks)

Choose the correct word to complete this conversation.

A: Could you e-mail me your latest price list?
B: Yes, one moment, *I / I'm / I'll* [1] just get a pen.
A: Ready?
B: Yes, *speak / go ahead / tell me* [2].
A: The company is Socotim. *Shall / Do / Will* [3] I spell that?
B: Yes, please.
A: That's S-O-C-O-T-I-M. Have you *note / write / got* [4] that?
B: Yes, I have. *Continue / I'm listening / Go on* [5].
A: And my e-mail address is phil@socotim.com.
B: *Please / Sorry / Pardon* [6]. Is that P–H–I–L?
A: Yes, that's *right / good / fine* [7].
B: And could I just *have / give / tell* [8] your full name?
A: Yes, it's Phil Styles. With a 'y'.
B: OK, Mr. Styles. I'll send that immediately. Was there anything else?
A: No, that's *good / finish / all* [9].

F Word families

(20 marks)

What is the noun form of the verbs below? Choose from the endings in the box.

| -ation | -ence | -ment | -ner | -er | -al | -ion |

Example: invite   *invitation*

1 retire   ....
2 dismiss   ....
3 resign   ....
4 recruit   ....
5 connect   ....
6 print   ....
7 scan   ....
8 develop   ....
9 prefer   ....
10 attach   ....

Now choose a verb or noun from the list to complete these sentences.

a The Personnel Officer is responsible for .... of staff.
b He decided to .... after only three months in the new post.
c I have a definite .... for the first of the two candidates.
d We have a very bad Internet .... , so documents take a long time to send.
e Our new spreadsheet program is only in the first stage of ....
f Please .... a copy of the original invoice to your cheque.

g I always use a laser .... because it's much faster.
h Would you like to take early .... when you are 55?
i If we .... the photo of the new factory, we can e-mail it to all our subsidiaries.
j He's taking legal advice because he thinks his .... from the company was against the law.

G Complaints
(10 marks)

Complete the sentences using an expression with *too* or *enough* and the word in brackets.
Example: He can't retire because he isn't *old enough* (old)

1 I can't drink this coffee because it's (strong) .... for me.
2 It's impossible to work in my office because it's (noisy) ....
3 The service in this restaurant is slow because there aren't (waiters) ....
4 He doesn't like flying in Economy Class because the seats aren't (wide) ....
5 He never goes by car because there is (traffic) .... on the roads in the morning.
6 She wants to change supplier because her present supplier's products are (expensive) ....
7 He lost his job because he made (mistakes) ....
8 We have to find a larger meeting room because this one isn't (big) .... for 30 people.
9 He's still in the same job because he isn't (ambitious) ....
10 I'll have to finish it on Monday because I don't have (time) .... today.

H A job interview
(16 marks)

You are at an interview for a job. Give short answers to the interviewer's questions (minimum three words), then add more information.

Examples: A: Are you a student?
 B: *No, I'm not. I have a full-time job.*
 A: Do you speak any other languages, apart from English?
 B: *Yes, I do. I speak French and German.*

1
A: Do you do any sport?
B: ....
2
A: Did you learn English at school?
B: ....
3
A: Are you taking any language lessons at the moment?
B: ....
4
A: Do you enjoy speaking English?
B: ....
5
A: Have you ever visited any English-speaking countries?
B: ....
6
A: Would you like to work abroad at some time in the future?
B: ....
7
A: Have you ever worked for a big company like ours?
B: ....
8
A: So will you be free to work for us next month?
B: ....

Progress test 5 (Units 1–12) 100 marks

A Past, present, and future
(10 marks)

Complete each sentence with the correct form of the verb in brackets.
Example: He can't come at the moment. He (speak) *is speaking* with a client.

1
 A: What are you doing next week?
 B: I (fly) .... to Prague for a big sales conference.
2 If we get the contract, we (be) .... in a very good position.
3
 A: What should we do with our guest this evening?
 B: He (like) .... music, so maybe we could go to the opera.
4 They usually deliver on Fridays, but this month they (deliver) .... on Wednesdays.
5 He (work) .... for this company since 1992.
6 Our sales (be) .... a lot higher last month.
7
 A: Do you know how this lock works?
 B: Wait just one moment. I (open) .... it for you.
8 I (not / call) .... you yesterday because I didn't have your number.
9 She works thirty-five hours a week, but she (not / work) .... on Fridays.
10 We (not / produce) .... anything at the moment – all the workers are on strike.

B Correct the mistake
(12 marks)

Correct the mistake in each sentence.
Example: Where ~~are~~ you work? *do*

1 He never work at weekends. ....
2 How much people does your company employ? ....
3 Pierre joined this company three years past. ....
4 There is three factories near Warsaw. ....
5 This product is expensiver than I thought. ....
6 He's worked here since three years. ....
7 It's the baddest job I've ever had. ....
8 A: How does it cost?
 B: Fifty dollars. ....
9 Our annual conference will be on March. ....
10 The security guard have to work at night. ....
11 If I won't have time today, I'll finish the report tomorrow. ....
12 Excuse me, sir. You don't have to park here, it's not permitted. ....

C Asking questions
(12 marks)

It is 9.30 a.m. on Friday. Study this page from Peter's diary.

Wednesday	6.00 p.m. Etta Jans (Draftex) arrives
Thursday	Presentation of quality programme to Etta Jans
Friday	With Etta Jans
	9.00 – 11.30 tour of factory
	12.30 Lunch
	15.00 Take Etta Jans to station

Now expand the notes to complete the questions, as in the example.
A: (be / Peter / here)
 Is Peter here? 1
B: No, he isn't. He's with a visitor, Etta Jans.
A: (Who / she / work / for?)
 2
B: For Draftex. She's the Purchasing Manager.
A: Oh yes, I remember. (What / he / do / with her / at the moment?)
 3
B: They're on a tour of the factory.
A: (How long / she / be / here?)
 4
B: Since Wednesday evening. She arrived about six.
A: (When / he / give / his presentation?)
 5
B: Yesterday. He says it went well.
A: That's good. Actually, I need to speak to Peter. (What time / Ms Jans / leave?)
 6

Progress Tests 91

B: Well, he's taking her to the station at three o' clock.
A: (he / be / free / after that?)
....
B: I think so.

D Telephoning for an appointment

(10 marks)

Choose the correct word or phrase to complete this dialogue.

A: Graphipac. Can I help you?
B: Yes. *I like to / I'd like to / Can I to* [1] speak to Morgane, please.
A: I'm *afraid / sorry / regret* [2], but Morgane is with a client at the moment. Can I *take / leave / give* [3] a message, or would you *like / want / have* [4] to call back later?
B: Is her assistant Tamsin there?
A: Yes, she is. Shall I put you *connect / in / through* [5] ?
B: Yes, please.
C: Hello, Tamsin speaking.
B: Hello, Tamsin. *Here is / I am / This is* [6] Greg. I wanted to *take / make / do* [7] an appointment with Morgane. Is she there tomorrow?
C: Let me just check, Greg … Yes, in fact she is here. *Is / Does / Can* [8] eleven o' clock suit you?
B: Well, the beginning of the afternoon would be more *suit / better / convenient* [9] .
C: *How / Is / If* [10] about two o' clock?
B: Yes, that's fine. So that's tomorrow at 2 p.m. then. Thanks, Tamsin.

E Confusing words

(10 marks)

The words underlined are not correct in these sentences. Replace them with the correct word.
Example: He always buys from us – he's one of our best competitors. ..*customers*..

1 Are you English ..*No, I'm not*..

1 (in a restaurant) I'd like to pay. Can you bring me the note, please? ....
2 We have 300 production workers in our manufacture. ....
3 Excuse me – is there a parking near here? ....
4 Can I present you to my boss, Mr Rivaldi? Mr Rivaldi, this is Duncan Ross. ....

5 How long did your travel to Paris take? ....
6 (at an airport) Excuse me, is this the register desk for the Sofia flight? ....
7 To relax at weekends, I like hearing music. ....
8 Do you product these yourselves, or do you buy them? ....
9 I'll look in my daybook, and see if I'm free next Thursday. ....
10 I'd like a double ticket to Frankfurt, please. ....

F Meetings

(12 marks)

1 Read these extracts from a meeting to discuss the recruitment of a new manager. Correct the mistake in each sentence, as in the examples.

a ~~Do we can discuss~~ recruitment now? *Can we discuss*
b I think we ~~should to offer~~ it to somebody in the company. *should offer*
c How do you think about that proposal, Martin? ....
d What about to advertise in the Sunday newspapers? ....
e Why we don't give the post to the Assistant Manager? ....
f Yes. Would you like that I start? ....
g I think we shouldn't do that – it's an unnecessary expense. ....
h I'm thinking he's too young at the moment. ....
i I'm not agree – there's nobody here who's really good enough. ....
j At my opinion, we should advertise inside and outside the company. ....

2 Now match a–e with f–j to form pairs of sentences, as in the example.

G Socializing

(12 marks)

Complete the questions for Person A and answers for Person B with polite expressions, as in the examples.

Person A	Person B
How are you?	*Fine, thanks. And you?*
Nice to see you again.	Nice to see you again too.
1 .... journey?	Yes, thanks, but I'm a little tired after my flight.

2 I'm sorry I'm late.   It ....
3 Thank you for meeting   ....
   me.
4 .... coffee?   Yes, please. No milk.
5 We're having a very good   I'm ....
   year.
6 .... take your coat?   Yes, please. That's very
                                        kind of you.

H Word groups
(15 marks)

Look at the words in the box. Add two of the words to each of the five groups (Company departments, Company jobs, etc.). Then complete the fourth word in each group.

Research	distributor	Chairman	interview
costs	Managing Director	shortlist	share price
Purchasing	sales outlet		

Company departments	Company jobs	Finding new staff
Sales	secretary	CV
....	....	....
....	....	....
Per............	acc............	cand............

A company works with ...	Company statistics
customer	profit
....	....
....	....
supp............	tur............

I Word pairs
(7 marks)

Choose one word from group A and one from group B to complete each sentence, as in the example.

A

| spreadsheet | product | interest | mail |
| job | parent | sales | market |

B

| rate | program | order | company |
| conference | range | share | applications |

1 Our annual *sales conference* was in June this year.
2 Our new .... includes two new models of computer for the family.
3 The company doesn't have any shops – it sells all its products by ....
4 This bank is offering an .... of 4.5%.
5 Our .... is now 30%. That's 5% more than our nearest competitors.
6 I work for a manufacturing subsidiary. Our .... is in the USA.
7 We have over 500 .... and we're going to start interviewing soon.
8 Every regional office uses the same .... for its accounts.

Answer key to tests

Test 1

A (1 mark for each correct answer)

1 'm
2 come
3 do
4 don't
5 have
6 export
7 is
8 aren't
9 travels
10 work
11 doesn't
12 are

B (2 marks for each correct answer)

2 Who do you work for?
3 What is the company's annual turnover?
4 How many rooms are there in the hotel?
5 Could you give me your name and telephone number?
6 What time does the next train leave?
7 Is there a plane to Tokyo this afternoon?

C (1 mark for each correct answer)

2 g
3 f
4 a
5 h
6 b
7 c
8 d
9 nineteen ninety-eight
10 one hundred and thirty-two euros (and) seventy (cents)
11 half past ten (or ten thirty) in the morning
12 seventy-eight thousand, three hundred (and) forty

D (1 mark for each correct answer)

1 to
2 from
3 to
4 opposite
5 on
6 On
7 to
8 at
9 to
10 by

E (1 mark for each correct answer)

1 Do
2 are
3 is
4 to
5 for
6 got
7 Do
8 bottles
9 to
10 would

F (1 mark for each correct word)

1 hold
2 message
3 starter, course, dessert
4 bill, receipt
5 single, shower
6 key, safe
7 head, based
8 employ, factory
9 check-in, ticket
10 lounge, control

G (1 mark for each correct answer)

1 f 3 g 5 a 7 h
2 b 4 e 6 c 8 d

H (1 mark for each correct answer)

2 Yes, (s)he is. / No, (s)he isn't. / No, (s)he's not.
3 Yes, (s)he does. / No, (s)he doesn't.
4 Yes, I am. / No, I'm not.
5 Yes, I do. / No, I don't.
6 Yes, it is. / No, it isn't. / No, it's not.
7 Yes, there are. / No, there aren't.
8 Yes, there is. / No, there isn't.
9 Yes, I do. / No, I don't.
10 Yes, I would. / No, I wouldn't.
11 Yes, I do. / No, I don't.

I (1 mark for each correct answer)

1 Excuse me
2 I'd like
3 Of course
4 would
5 Can
6 afraid
7 Could
8 afraid

Test 2

A (1 mark for each correct answer)

2 left
3 took
4 got
5 am staying
6 visited
7 went
8 am going
9 am flying
10 am seeing
11 met

B (1 mark for each correct answer)

2 12th September
3 Thursday
4 half past ten / 10.30 a.m.
5 4th September
6 August
7 October
8 eleven o'clock / 11.00 a.m.
9 a quarter to nine / 8.45 a.m.

C (1 mark for each correct answer)

2 manufacture, factory
3 turnover
4 recruit
5 product
6 employees, Division
7 accounts
8 customer, production
9 parent company, subsidiaries
10 competitors
11 advertise
12 training
13 Purchasing
14 suppliers

D (1 mark for each correct answer)

2 Where were you?
3 Where did you stay?
4 Do you know Prague?
5 What is she doing there?
6 What are you doing here today?
7 Do you know Peter Gordon?
8 What does he do?
9 When did you arrive?
10 What are you doing this evening?
11 Would you like to eat out somewhere?

E (1 mark for each correct answer)

1 g
2 i
3 h
4 j
5 f
6 c
7 a
8 b
9 e
10 d

F (2 marks for each correct answer)

2 No, it isn't. It's increasing.
3 No, they didn't. They rose.
4 No, they aren't. They're falling.
5 No, it didn't. It went up.
6 No, it didn't. It rose.

G (1 mark for each correct answer)

1 I'm / I am afraid he's not here this afternoon.
2 My boss is travelling to the Czech Republic on Thursday.
3 I arrived on Saturday at six o'clock.
4 She's a research scientist with Roche.
5 There are two secretaries in this department.
6 I work very hard so in the evening I like to relax.
7 I'd like to speak to Mr Taylor, please.
8 How long are you staying? Just three days?
9 I usually have lunch between one and two o'clock

H (1 mark for each correct word)

1 on, to, At, For
2 about, after, in
3 to, By, in

I (1 mark for each correct answer)

2 Could I speak to Bill Farrar, please?
3 I'm afraid he's not here today.
4 Then could you put me through to his assistant, Tamsin Rossiter?
5 I'm afraid her line's busy. Can I take a message?
6 No, that's OK, thanks. When is Mr Farrar due back?
7 Tomorrow morning, I think.
8 OK, I'll call back tomorrow.
9 Thank you for calling. Goodbye.

J (1 mark for each correct answer)

2 lives   6 spends
3 journey   7 attends
4 has   8 customers
5 travels   9 people

Test 3

A (1 mark for each correct answer)

1 most frequent   8 more dangerous
2 nicer   9 as good
3 faster   10 worst
4 cleaner   11 best
5 cheaper   12 most convenient
6 best   13 biggest
7 friendliest

B (1 mark for each correct answer)

1 was founded   5 were made
2 studied   6 acquired
3 started   7 won
4 was introduced   8 was built

C (1 mark for each correct answer)

1 When was he born?
2 Why did they cancel the meeting?
3 Could you look into the problem?
4 What are you doing next week?
5 What will you do if the hotel is full?
6 What is the longest bridge in the world?
7 Why are they building a new factory?
8 What is the best restaurant in the town?
9 How much does it weigh?
10 When was the company founded?
11 Shall I send you another copy?
12 Can you call me back?
13 What is your view on this?
14 What is the best way to travel to Paris?

D (1 mark for each correct pair of words)

1 shopping centre
2 fast / slow, relaxing / stressful, safe / dangerous, interesting / boring, easy / difficult, long / short
3 expand / expansion, acquire / acquisition, create / creation, weigh / weight
4 radio adverts, direct mailing
5 business people, general public

E (1 mark for each correct answer)

1 e   3 i   5 g   7 h   9 f
2 j   4 b   6 a   8 c   10 d

F (1 mark for each correct answer)

1 I think it**'ll** / **will** rain later today.
2 The restaurant is full, I**'m** / **am** afraid. Would you like to eat later?
3 Sparkling wine is not **as** expensive as champagne.
4 Mrs Lingwood arrived ten minutes **ago**.
5 If you advertise I think you will sell **a** lot.
6 I**'ll** / **will** call you back tomorrow morning.
7 Wimbledon is **the** most famous tennis tournament in the world.

8 I'm very sorry **about** that.
9 We'll be late **if** we don't leave now.
10 I look forward **to** meeting you next week.

G (1 mark for each correct answer)

1 round   5 clear   9 about
2 plastic   6 compact disc   10 weighs
3 thick   7 rectangular   11 black
4 square   8 wide   12 video-cassette

H (1 mark for each correct word)

1 founded, *accept correct number*
2 won, ago
3 following / next, became
4 had
5 died, *accept correct number*

I (1 mark for each correct answer)

1 customers   4 salary   7 profit
2 loan   5 loss   8 shares
3 interest rate 6 save   9 borrow

Test 4

A (1 mark for each correct answer)

1 do   6 should
2 employ   7 can't
3 don't   8 must
4 don't   9 offering
5 don't think 10 have to

B (2 marks for each correct answer)

In 2 and 3, accept correct number between now and year mentioned.

1 They moved here twenty years ago.
2 I've worked for my company for X* years.
3 I became Sales Director X* years ago.
4 He's been here for two days.
5 She's had this job for two years.
6 We started this business in 1998.

C (1 mark for each correct answer)

1 advertisement   6 experience
2 energetic   7 apply
3 ambitious   8 application
4 joined   9 interview
5 post / position 10 hearing

D (1 mark for each correct answer)

1 enjoy   6 Can   11 have to
2 have to   7 have to   12 enjoy
3 hate   8 allowed   13 don't have to
4 can   9 can
5 have to   10 mind

E (2 marks for each correct answer)

1 I'll   4 got   7 right
2 go ahead   5 Go on   8 have
3 Shall   6 Sorry   9 all

F (1 mark for each correct answer)

1 retirement   a recruitment
2 dismissal   b resign
3 resignation   c preference
4 recruitment   d connection
5 connection   e development
6 printer   f attach
7 scanner   g printer
8 development   h retirement
9 preference   i scan
10 attachment   j dismissal

G (1 mark for each correct answer)

1 too strong   6 too expensive
2 too noisy   7 too many mistakes
3 enough waiters   8 big enough
4 wide enough   9 ambitious enough
5 too much traffic 10 enough time

H (1 mark for each short answer, 1 mark for a logical and correct follow-up sentence)

1 Yes, I do. / No, I don't.
2 Yes, I did. / No, I didn't.
3 Yes, I am. / No, I'm not.
4 Yes, I do. / No, I don't.
5 Yes, I have. / No, I haven't.
6 Yes, I would. / No, I wouldn't.
7 Yes, I have. / No, I haven't.
8 Yes, I will. / No, I won't.

Test 5

A (1 mark for each correct answer)

1 'm flying / am flying
2 'll be / will be
3 likes
4 're / are delivering
5 's worked / has worked
6 were
7 'll open / will open
8 didn't call
9 doesn't / does not work
10 aren't / am not producing

B (1 mark for each correct answer)

1 He never *works* at weekends.
2 How *many* people does your company employ?
3 Pierre joined this company three years *ago*.
4 There *are* three factories near Warsaw.
5 This product is *more expensive* than I thought.
6 He's worked here *for* three years.
7 It's the *worst* job I've ever had.
8 How *much* does it cost?
9 Our annual conference will be *in* March.
10 The security guard *has* to work at night.
11 If I *don't* have time today, I'll finish the report tomorrow.
12 Excuse me, sir. You *mustn't* park here, it's not permitted.

Answer key   95

C (2 marks for each correct answer)

2 Who does she work for?
3 What's he doing with her at the moment?
4 How long has she been here?
5 When did he give his presentation?
6 What time is Ms Jans leaving?
7 Will he be / Is he free after that?

D (1 mark for each correct answer)

1 I'd like to
2 sorry
3 take
4 like
5 through
6 This is
7 make
8 Does
9 convenient
10 How

E (1 mark for each correct answer)

1 bill
2 factory / plant / company
3 car park
4 introduce
5 journey / trip / flight
6 check-in (registration)
7 listening to
8 produce / manufacture / make
9 diary
10 return

F (1 mark for each correct answer)

1 c What do you think … / How do you feel …?
  d What about advertising …?
  e Why don't we give …?
  f Would you like me to start?
  g I don't think we should do that …
  h I think …
  i I don't agree …
  j In my opinion …

2 bi cj dg eh

G (2 marks for each correct answer)

1 Did you have a nice / pleasant / good …?
2 It doesn't matter / 's not important.
3 You're welcome / It's a pleasure / Not at all.
4 Would you like some / a coffee?
5 I'm pleased / happy to hear that.
6 May I / Can I / Could I / Would you like me to …?

H (1 mark for each word in its correct category)

Company departments: Purchasing, Research, Personnel

Company jobs: Chairman, Managing Director, accountant

Finding new staff: shortlist, interview, candidate

A company works with … : distributor, sales outlet, supplier

Company statistics: costs, share price, turnover

I (1 mark for each correct answer)

2 product range
3 mail order
4 interest rate
5 market share
6 parent company
7 job applications
8 spreadsheet program